Widows Peek

Renette Torres
Courtney McEntee
Lynn Nilsen
Shirley Chapman
Helma Smith
Marlene Bolla
Stefi Rudolph
Becky Funk
Mona Wolters
Velma Tiffany

BALBOA
PRESS
A DIVISION OF HAY HOUSE

Copyright © 2013 Renette Torres et al.

All rights reserved. No part of this book may be used or reproduced by any means, graphic, electronic, or mechanical, including photocopying, recording, taping or by any information storage retrieval system without the written permission of the publisher except in the case of brief quotations embodied in critical articles and reviews.

Balboa Press books may be ordered through booksellers or by contacting:

*Balboa Press
A Division of Hay House
1663 Liberty Drive
Bloomington, IN 47403
www.balboapress.com
1-(877) 407-4847*

Because of the dynamic nature of the Internet, any web addresses or links contained in this book may have changed since publication and may no longer be valid. The views expressed in this work are solely those of the authors and do not necessarily reflect the views of the publisher, and the publisher hereby disclaims any responsibility for them.

The authors of this book does not dispense medical advice or prescribe the use of any technique as a form of treatment for physical, emotional, or medical problems without the advice of a physician, either directly or indirectly. The intent of the author is only to offer information of a general nature to help you in your quest for emotional and spiritual well-being. In the event you use any of the information in this book for yourself, which is your constitutional right, the author and the publisher assume no responsibility for your actions.

*Any people depicted in stock imagery provided by Thinkstock are models, and such images are being used for illustrative purposes only.
Certain stock imagery © Thinkstock.*

*ISBN: 978-1-4525-7006-8 (sc)
ISBN: 978-1-4525-7008-2 (hc)
ISBN: 978-1-4525-7007-5 (e)*

Library of Congress Control Number: 2013904220

Printed in the United States of America

Balboa Press rev. date: 03/15/2013

Acknowledgments

This book is the collaborated effort of nine ladies who came together to tell the story of their own personal experience with widowhood. Without the courage and willingness of these women to write and have their stories read in print throughout the world, for the sole purpose of helping other widows get through the terrible void that is left after losing their loved one, Widows Peek would not have been possible.

My congratulations and heartfelt thanks to each of my authors for making this book a reality. It feels so good to help other women get over the bumps and ruts on the lonely road that lies ahead, to lift the dark veil, and to go forward and spiral up.

Also by Renette Torres: *Ya Wanna Watch? I'll Let Ya!*
Visit Renette's website at: http://renettetorres.com

Contents

Preface: Renette Torres 1

Chapter 1:   Renette's Story 5

Chapter 2:   Courtney's Story..37

Chapter 3:   Lynn's Story 41

Chapter 4:   Shirley's Story 55

Chapter 5:   Helma's Story 63

Chapter 6:   Marlene's Story..73

Chapter 7:   Stefi's Story 91

Chapter 8:   Becky's Story 99

Chapter 9:   Mona's Story.. 109

Chapter 10: Velma's Story.. 133

Inner Views: Renette Torres.. 149

Preface
Renette Torres

You are probably asking why I wanted to compile a book about widows and their stories. The answer is simple—because I am a widow myself, I wanted to help others going through the same huge void I was going through. Indeed, this is a unique book. It's an observation of how these women have risen above and gotten through this terrible lonely ordeal. After you meet these ladies by reading their individual stories, their illuminating backgrounds, with a description of what each woman went through; you will learn the real meaning of courage and strength. I believe there is enough varied information from these stories to give solace as well as hope to those who are newly widowed or even long-term widows who still have not been able to pick up the pieces and have not yet been successful in putting their lives back on track. I truly hope this book will bring some comfort, helping to make the going easier in a tough time. We all experience the feeling of loneliness, but you are NOT alone!

When I formulated the idea of a book about women who have lost their husbands, I decided to make a list of the people I knew personally who lost their guys. I began to list the names and phone numbers on a sheet of paper. To my complete surprise, I had a total of 29 names, including my own. That's a lot of widows of all ages.

How could I get these people together? Would they be interested in sharing stories of their married lives, their background, and the loneliness they were feeling? And how are they surviving now?

I decided to invite all the women to a dessert and coffee afternoon at my home here at Ridgemark. Most of the ladies live here or close by. I sent emails or called by phone to give them the particulars of the upcoming party.

It was set for a particular Wednesday at 2:00 in the afternoon. To my complete surprise, all except five showed up at my front door. I welcomed each lady individually and told them to help themselves to the dessert and coffee or tea in the kitchen, and then come into the living room to meet and talk with the other women. I thought it would be nice to have everyone introduce themselves.

While they were eating their dessert and sipping coffee I told them we were all members of the same club, I explained that we were having a "Widows Peek" party, and that I would confess to why I invited all of them there that day.

"How can you and I help other widows everywhere? Why don't WE write a book describing our own personal experiences? It will be a collective effort. Each widow must write her own chapter." I certainly could feel the excitement rising up in all of them. Me, too!

I told the assembled group, "Here is some information I will pass out to each of you. This is the base for your widow's story. Each of you will write your own story, which will become a chapter in our book entitled *Widows Peek*." Most of them seemed very excited with interest mounting in what was going to be a most illustrious and different type of book.

I handed out the sheet of paper that sketched out the story base for our book. It contained simple instructions, mostly in outline form, of what was required for their chapter. It was a delightful afternoon. They left with something new and different to think about, which was a good thing in itself. I always say try to think of new things to do. It'll keep your brain busy, which is also a very good thing.

Some of the ladies, after I talked to them individually later, opted for one reason or another not to participate. Some said: "I'm not a good writer," others, "I feel too sad when I think about all of that," or "We didn't have an interesting life." Most of these people had never written anything before. I continued to urge some of them to try it, and see what happens. I had definitely nine to ten women who agreed to write their story for the book you are about to read.

True, there is sadness. You will feel the pain, of course, but will also revel in the strength and vigor of these women as they relate their stories. There is humor. There is love. There are also strange occurrences. However, first and foremost, there is remembering—the good memories and the not-so-good memories. I think everyone will agree that physical exercise is good for our bodies, but as reflected here, exercising our minds has been even more exhilarating. My authors and I are certain you will be inspired once you have absorbed the wisdom and experiences contained herein.

Chapter 1

Renette's Story

Where do I start to tell you about the beginning of the end?

Someone once said to me that a heart attack and mandatory retirement are the beginning of the end. I have always thought it was a new beginning, and so it was! I am going to tell you just a little about the real beginning.

I will go back in time briefly in order for you to get a glimpse of Danny and me. Danny was born in New York City to Rose Alhadeff Torres and David Torres; he was the oldest of four children. His siblings were all born in California. My mother-in-law, Rose, was a quiet, petite, pretty lady born on the Isle of Rhodes, one of the many beautiful islands owned by Greece. My father-in-law was born in Salonika, on the mainland of Greece (because of the very long drive, it's one of the few places on our vast planet Danny and I never visited). He was a charming-soft spoken, nice-looking man who adored his family. His occupation was a florist.

Rose and her two brothers came to the United States before World War II. Somehow, despite the war, she received news from Rhodes about her relatives. Much later, after Danny and I were married, she told me a story that made chills run up my spine. She somehow heard a horrific story about when the Germans occupied her beautiful island during WW II, the Nazis chained all her relatives (and many others, too) into small boats, and after riddling the boats with bullets, sent them to their doom in the Mediterranean Sea. You may ask, why did this happen? The Nazi regime tried to get rid of all Jews from the countries they occupied.

Danny's parents were Sephardic Jews, whose ancestors emigrated from Spain to Greece, and so his ancestors were all originally from Spain. During the Spanish Inquisition, the Jewish people were forced to join the Catholic Church or leave the country, and if they stayed and didn't convert to Catholicism they were killed. The expulsion of the Jews from Spain took place in 1492, a terrible time in the history of mankind.

It was in New York City that Rose met David, (They never knew each other in Greece.) They married and had their first child Danny there, in 1923, then journeyed to California when he was two years old. The Torres family settled in Oakland. As a young man, Danny served as a navigator in the US Army Air Corps during the war. Danny later graduated from University of California, Berkeley with a degree in Accounting and Business Administration.

I was born June 14, 1929, in San Francisco, that year was the beginning of the Great Depression. My mother, Renée, was an only child born to Max and Henrietta Levy. She was very spoiled, and most definitely a snob. My grandparents, as I recall, were very social, and fun-loving people. Grandma, with her outgoing personality, had lots of friends, unlike my mother, who was cold, self-centered, always had a negative attitude, and was extremely difficult to get along with.

My dad was an attorney named Harold Abraham. He specialized in criminal law and was well known throughout the San Francisco criminal court system. After school I would sometimes go to the courthouse, just to see and hear him in action. He always told me I had a great gift of gab and said I would make a good trial lawyer and could train in his law office. Dad and I had a special relationship. He was smart, warm, loving, and had a great time joking around. He always enjoyed a good laugh, and all of my friends adored him. On the other hand, none of my friends liked my mother who was cold with a rigid demeanor, for example; she never allowed her children to call her "Mom" We had to call her "Mother." She thought the word mom was disrespectful.

San Francisco is where my two brothers and I grew up. I played girls' basketball, volleyball, and was active in the Silver Blades, a speed-skating club that skated on the ice at the famous Sutro Baths. Unfortunately, that landmark has long been torn down.

After I graduated high school in San Francisco, we moved to Piedmont, a small, affluent city in the East Bay, and I attended the California College of Arts and Crafts, and graduated with a BA degree in Liberal Arts. I joined a young person's group called "Guys and Gals," a social group of young people that met once a month, located in Oakland, where Danny lived. I had seen him there but we never spoke.

The first time I actually met and talked with Danny was on a blind date with his brother, Jack, and my friend Barbara Berman. We went to the Grand Lake Theater to see "Oliver Twist." The year was 1951. Danny seemed quiet, very intelligent, but a little shy. He was definitely a handsome young guy. We saw each other frequently thereafter and after several months of getting to know each other, he proposed to me. At that time, I was also seeing a young man named Ivan, who was from Los Angeles, and an heir to a large pasta company. He was "rich" and hung out with his close friends, Tony Curtis and Piper Laurie—you know, the Hollywood set.

He had nothing on me, I was friends with Shirley Temple and would see her every Easter vacation at her home in the Desert Inn in Palm Springs. My folks and her folks enjoyed mutual friends that owned the Wonder Date Garden and one of the largest orange groves in that area. My dad raised Great Danes for stud purposes and, showed them at dog shows; Shirley was enamored with them. Shirley and I were the same age, around twelve when we met. We wrote to each other often.

My mother loved Ivan because he brought her gifts, and she preferred the wealthy boy to Danny, who was from a family of modest income, (Remember, I told you she was a snob!) When I first met Danny, he was working at The House of Flowers in San Francisco as a florist, and he was also their accountant. This shop had no connection with his father's flower shop in Oakland, although Danny had worked in his father's business from the age of eight. At the same time he also delivered newspapers by bicycle with childhood friends who later would become his "poker club" after high school, college and the military service. They met every month their entire adult life. There are now only two guys left out of a group of eight lifelong friends.

Danny never brought my mother any gifts, like Ivan had done. Her nose was so far up in the air it made me sick. She didn't care for Danny (he didn't come from wealth!) She really wanted me to marry Ivan, who had a very outgoing personality. Danny was quiet, a deep thinker, serious minded, exceptionally smart and had a calm disposition, much better for me because I was the comic—constantly talking, always kidding around and having fun. I loved to make him laugh. He was my "straight" man.

Despite my mother's objections, Danny and I married in April, 1952. We began our life together in a little apartment in Oakland; we lived there for six months, and then bought a tract-house in Pleasant Hill in the East Bay.

Later, after the completion of our custom-built home in Burton Valley, an upscale neighborhood in Lafayette, California, we resided there for 14 years. We raised three children: Kenny, Cathy, and Rhonda. We had a fabulous social life there. Tennis was our passion, and, being avid players, we joined Round Hill Country Club in Alamo, where we had a huge circle of friends. It seemed we were always partying.

Our residential journey in 1975, after the children were out of school, was to continue south to the Almaden Valley. Danny was Chief Financial Officer of a super market company called Nob Hill Foods; the corporate offices were located in Gilroy, a lengthy commute from Lafayette. The move to Almaden would make the commute shorter. There we joined the Saratoga Golf and Country Club, where we played tennis and again had a huge group we socialized with. Danny and I also belonged to Carmel Valley Racquet Club, where we would go every weekend we were in town, to play nine sets of tennis every Saturday, and nine sets on Sunday. We did that so often, we decided to buy a condo in Forest Grove (Pacific Grove). It was easier to stay in our own place rather than a hotel. It was always spectacular down there. The people were fabulous and it was great getting away on weekends! Such fun and energetic times! We were always "on the go." You might say we enjoyed "the club life."

Only twenty-one years ago
Our "moving south" journey continued to Ridgemark Golf and Country Club in Hollister, about forty-five miles east of Carmel-by-the-Sea. This would be only a twenty minute commute for Danny to drive to his Gilroy office. It was at Ridgemark that we built a lovely home overlooking the seventh fairway of one

of the two beautiful golf courses, where the weather is always fantastic.

I still had my "It's Time" watch and clock business, which I started in 1981. I was on the road most of the time, designing, importing and marketing to all the major department stores across the nation, hotels, gambling casinos, and so many other businesses. Danny and I were traveling often by this time—business trips for him as well as watch fairs for me in Basal, Switzerland, and Hong Kong.

Though Ridgemark had two lovely golf courses, we were not fans of the golfing scene yet, that would happen later . . . there was plenty of time for that. Also available were six new tennis courts, just perfect for us. We planned to move in September 1990. Danny, had a heart attack in June of 1990, and was in frail condition. I had to have a second arthroscopic knee surgery. Despite our physical conditions, we moved into our new home. The weather in this central California location is almost perfect, a very well kept secret. Many people think it is too hot; actually it has nice warm days and cool evenings, an ideal temperature most of the year for tennis, golf and outdoor living. I've always called it "God's little acre."

Danny shared his high-level position with an energetic, innovative board of directors. There were nine in all, of which Danny was a crucial part. Danny, because of his financial position, was called the "NO" man, doing what he liked best, controlling the finances. We were stockholders of the company, so Danny kept a keen eye on the monies spent for the company as well as the park.

Michael, the CEO, built a fantastic employee's park. It was beautiful. It included two tennis courts, an Olympic-size swimming pool, an exercise room, barbeque facilities, and gorgeous gardens. Basketball courts adorned a modern gymnasium where the corporate officers team, Danny included, played the different store's basketball teams. It was fun cheering on our guys. We often invited friends down on weekends to play mixed doubles. We barbequed after playing tennis, it was such fun. Our friends always wanted to be asked again. Michael called this fantastic employee park "Tree Haven." It was, indeed a haven.

Michael went on to build a theme park with a huge lake, rides for children including a train, and many restaurants for families to come and enjoy. It was extremely costly! It is now a huge tourist attraction and owned by the city of Gilroy.

What a birthday!
It was June 14, 1990 (my birthday) at almost 3:00 in the afternoon. I had just gotten home from an exciting sales appointment with a large industrial corporation that wanted their logo on several styles of my watches and clocks. I was thinking "what a great birthday present." That order really made my day, but my bubble was soon to burst.

It was just a few months prior to moving from Almaden to Ridgemark, when the phone rang. I picked it up and, trying to be funny, I said, "It's your nickel, shoot!" To my surprise it was Danny on the other end of the line, saying, "Renette, now don't be alarmed—I've had a heart attack. I'm at Good Samaritan Hospital in the cardiac unit. Don't worry—I'm plugged in and they tell me I'm doing fine."

Danny was a very soft spoken, always calm, and easy-going kind of guy, but his conversation was labored and extremely weak. That frightened me. I picked up my car keys, hurriedly flew into the garage, jumped in, and started the car. I drove to the hospital, being very worried about my husband and if he was really okay like he had told me. This was not the sort of birthday present I expected, nor wanted.

When I walked into the hospital, I very nervously asked one of the pink ladies where the cardiac area was. I stopped at the nurses' station and asked again if anyone knew where Dan Torres was. They directed me to his bed in the heart unit. I walked in and there he was, all wired up, with a flashing heart monitor lit up, tubes and IVs everywhere. I bent down and gave him a soft kiss. He opened his eyes and gave me his sweet smile. I tried hard to hold back the tears, and then I felt a hand on my shoulder, and turning around, it was our doctor. He motioned to me to follow him out of the room to the hallway. He then told me of Danny's condition. He explained the attack was serious but assured me he would be fine, with proper diet, therapy and exercise. He also said Danny must retire from his CFO position at Nob Hill Foods. It was a job that he loved so much, but evidently the responsibility and importance of his position weighed heavily on him without his realizing it, and gave him too much stress.

Life changes
I returned home from the ordeal of Danny's heart attack late in the evening. The sight of him, so pale, and plugged into all the monitors, plus the worrisome stress I had been given that day left me totally exhausted. I bent down and hugged our two black and white Shih Tzu dogs, Chip and Dale, then absolutely collapsed into a chair in the den, and fell fast asleep. I was startled awake by a telephone call from the cardiologist telling me that he was going to do an invasive procedure on Danny that evening to unclog his artery. He said if I wanted to be there, then I should come right away. It was 10:00 p.m. then, but I grabbed my keys and jumped back into the car and drove to the hospital. When I arrived, they were just taking him into the surgical unit. I kissed him and said I would be there when he woke up. He was in a dopey state, so I didn't know if he realized I was even there. I went and got a cup of coffee, my head reeling from the day's events. I fell asleep in the waiting room and awakened when I felt the

doctor touch my hand. He told me Danny was fine and that I should go home and rest. Breathing a sigh of relief, I drove home and went to bed.

The morning after his heart procedure, I called to find out how he was. The nurse said he was resting. When I got to the hospital, poor Danny had a very heavy brick wrapped in a towel placed on his groin area. Evidently they had a dynamite time trying to stop the bleeding from the incision they had to make, to insert the tube into the artery that goes into the heart. After several days in the hospital, he was ready to come home and begin his new life. I was told that he may become depressed, but that goes away soon. Danny never was depressed. He was always so cool and calm about everything, even his own heart condition.

With proper eating habits, several weeks of exercise and therapy at the hospital rehab unit, we would be able to resume our normal life style minus his job at Nob Hill Foods. When the time was right, he would be interviewing candidates for his Financial Vice President's position, the candidate to be approved by the Board of Directors.

A healthy specimen
Danny had always been very healthy and in superb physical shape, even as he aged. He was a basketball player when he was young. He had strong arms and legs, a bit hairy, had a great physique, very nice looking with a healthy head of hair. What I called my "Hard-Body." He was very attractive and people we met all over the world would often comment about how much he looked like Spencer Tracy. He looked terrific in his tennis shorts and was such a handsome man when he wore his tuxedo. He looked good in everything he put on, even a Japanese kimono he had to sport on one of our trips to Japan at a dinner party with some Japanese friends. He looked just as great without clothes.

The only other time I remembered that he had to go to the hospital was when he had kidney stones, and I remember how much pain he was in then. He had the flu occasionally, and once had a slight case of the shingles, but got rid of them quickly. He was very lucky. One time on a business trip to Hong Kong, he complained he didn't feel very well, and thought he had the "Hong Kong" flu so Catherine Lam, the woman who owned the watch factory I did business with, told Danny she was taking him to the hospital. The Chinese doctor at the hospital, who spoke excellent English, said to Danny, "You don't have the Hong Kong flu, you have the US flu." We all laughed, thought it was really funny. Whatever flu bug it was, he got over it quickly.

Retired, but not expired
Danny was doing well, and was back to playing tennis, maybe not quite as vigorously as before, but still a top "A" club player. When we played doubles, because he was a lefty, he always had me playing the backhand court, the left side, close to the net. I'm right-handed, thus our strength was always down the middle, and we were a good competitive team. After we were settled in our Ridgemark home, we played tennis several times a week. We still had our weekend condo in Pacific Grove, and were still playing at the Carmel Valley Racquet Club on weekends. I played on the ladies' inter-club team for five years. Danny played on the men's ladder. Soon, however, we did start playing golf. I really liked it (today, I am obsessed), but he hated it. Danny decided to buy a mountain bike and explore San Benito County's beautiful countryside. He would ride for hours. He would come home and tell me how beautiful it was and how fantastic he felt after several hours sitting on that tiny little seat. Shortly after discovering the scenic hills and terrain of our area, he invested in a road bike, making him go faster, and, it had an even smaller seat. It actually was a racing bike.

I could not just play golf; I had to get busy with other things. My "It's Time" business was starting up again. That is when I started my mail-order business from home. This was good for Danny as well. He had some financial challenges again, this time for a home-grown business. I could see he loved it, and it put the light back in his eyes. Guess retirement isn't the end of the world, after all. Speaking of the world, we traveled a lot when we were both working in our respective fields, but we began to take three trips a year after retiring. We both loved to cruise the high seas all over the world. We took 32 cruises, and almost as many land tours. Our passports were filled rapidly with the colorful little inked stamps each country placed on the pages. We particularly loved the Mediterranean area, visiting the Greek Isles eight times. We both were interested in ancient history and loved the archeological sites we visited: Ephesus, just outside Kushadasi, Turkey, and a new "dig," Akotiri, on the other side of Santorini, which sits in a volcanic bowl, one of the most interesting of the Greek islands.

Aside from all the world traveling we did, we flew to Hawaii every year. We loved all the islands, but early on, we often stayed at the corporate condo in Kauai at Kiahuna, a golf and tennis resort. We stayed at Princeville several times as well as Kapalua resort on Maui, but our favorite was the Hilton Waikoloa, on the Kona side of the big island. We went there every October for 25 years, and stayed in the same room in the Lagoon Tower overlooking the dolphin training pond. Everyone there knew us well, and the trainers would call us at home when one of the pregnant dolphins had a baby. They would say to us, "You're grandparents again!"

Some memory lapses
I was very much into golfing, because Danny and I were no longer playing tennis. He would help out at the triathlon each year near our hotel on the big island. I took my golf clubs and

being a single, let the pro shop set me up to make a foursome. I always met nice people that way.

I had noticed Danny would lose his memory of certain things once in awhile, but really didn't think much about it. I spoke to the concierge at our tower and also notified the main lobby personnel that if they saw him wandering around, looking like he was lost, to please take him to our room. I guess I had a feeling that something was not right with him, so that's why I notified those employees. Well, when I returned from golf I was told that after he went across the bridge to get some lunch at Hang Ten, a little snack shack near the pool, he couldn't find his way back, and didn't recall what room he was in. Thank goodness I alerted them earlier. Was it intuition?

Disneyland to Alaska
In April 2005, after planning a September cruise to Alaska, which would be our final adventure, we decided to drive down to southern California. We visited our friends, the Ritchie's, who lived in Tustin. We spent a whole day with them, and after having an early dinner, we drove to the Disneyland Hotel where we had stayed with our children many years prior. It was our anniversary. I noticed Danny was somewhat disoriented and was asking me strange questions about his car. We drove my car and his car was home in the garage. He kept asking me where the "folder" was. I continued to be shaken up by his weird questions about his car and a "folder." We had an okay time watching the people and going on our favorite rides. I became alarmed as well as baffled with so many of the strange remarks Danny was making. As soon as we got home, I called our doctor and made an appointment for him. He worried me.

A heart like his dad . . . a brain like his mom
He was tested for Dementia/Alzheimer's disease, and the tests came out positive. His gray matter was obviously deteriorating

at a very fast speed. Danny was always so smart, so intelligent, and so world.ly-wise, he could answer any question you put in front of him. Danny was at this point 82 years old. He had been drinking more and the doctor said that was a big contributing factor to the problem. Alcohol was eating his brain, but Danny loved his cocktails and, as hard as I tried, I could not make him stop drinking. We would be going to the doctors more often in the coming months. His mom had dementia. It was heart wrenching to watch her, even worse watching him.

Alaskan cruising . . . and still boozing
I always said the last cruise Danny and I would go on would be to Alaska. It was. We had a gorgeous suite, complete with a balcony. At dinner we had a table for ten—that was always our favorite number for dinner. We always seemed to meet such great people on our cruises. I still keep in touch with so many of them through email. On that trip, we met four British people, two Canadians, and a couple from the USA. I planned a cocktail party and ordered liquor (just what Danny didn't need) and lots of appetizers. It was our second-to-last night at sea, and I thought we should have a final tribute to our sailing days (maybe now sailing daze), and the party turned out great. Everyone had a good time. Danny was even making the cocktails and making conversation, even jokes, with our guests. To observe him, he looked and acted perfectly normal. I think I was dreaming! We had a great time.

A five-hour bike ride!
Danny was still riding his bike around the countryside and seemed to still know where he was going. One day I looked at the clock and thought, where the heck is he, he left almost five hours ago. OMG, did he get disoriented again? Is he lost? It was an extremely hot day, but Danny always had plenty of water with him. The doorbell rang and as I opened the door, a young man was helping Danny inside our entry hall.

He looked painfully exhausted. This nice guy found Danny sitting on a curb by the side of the road. The driver stopped and asked if he could take him home. Danny agreed. He knew where he lived—a good sign! He didn't think he was biking that long. I wish everyone was as nice as that concerned man was.

After that episode, Danny would just ride around Ridgemark. That bothered him because now I was restricting him, taking over, so to speak. Danny always made his own decisions. This was not a good thing. I felt terrible as I was taking away one of his few pleasures left. It made me sad.

The heart of the matter
Because of Danny's coronary troubles, I took him to his heart specialist every couple of months. He would get lost going thirty-five miles south to Salinas by himself, so I would take the wheel. I wanted to hear what his cardiologist was telling him, anyway. Danny had three more angioplasty surgeries, and one more stent. We stuck pretty close to home. He and I would go to the symphony and light opera series, which we both enjoyed through the years. One year, I recall, we flew to New York just to go to the Broadway shows. We loved it. We used to go and do so much together, but Danny wasn't enjoying it anymore. Nearby restaurants and the movies was "our thing" now. I used to tell everyone Danny and I were going on a "date!"

He wasn't biking anymore. He was doing nothing, just sitting staring at the TV. He did nothing on his computer either. He used to be glued to it. Did he know what he was watching on television? Did he know what was happening? I could not tell because I didn't know either. I felt I was losing my darling Danny, and there was nothing I could do about it. I felt totally helpless! The last several months of Danny's life were excruciating for me. He complained about his feet hurting, and he said it was hard to walk. The doctor told us he had an extremely bad case of gout and prescribed pills . . . which did nothing! He was failing rapidly, mentally and physically. He was sent to a foot surgeon, given more pills but to no avail. His condition was getting worse.

I thought to myself, first the heart, next the mind, and now the feet. Poor Danny, nothing helped. People said to try cherry juice so he drank tons of that. No improvement!

Danny's deterioration prompted Renette's inspiration

About six months prior to Danny's passing, I decided I needed something for my brain other than golf. I felt so low and helpless, I would even break out in tears on the golf course while I was with my friends, but my mind was always at home with Danny, not really concentrating on my golf game. It was difficult for me to think about anything but him. He took all my energy. I wanted so much to help him, but the only thing I could do was just watch him going downhill.

Feeling the strain—needing work for my brain

I was really feeling the strain from a completely lost battle, and a sense of total defeat. "I have never given up and I will not now!" I thought to myself, as I was reflecting back over our almost 56 wonderful years together as husband and wife, as lovers, as best friends, as parents, grand-parents, as traveling companions, dancing partners—what a remarkable life I've had with Danny. I sat down at my computer and leaned my head back, closed my eyes, and thought to myself, "Renette, you have had such a colorful and exciting life with Danny. Think how supportive he was for your watch and clock business, all the parties, so many fabulous trips all over the world, our network of friends and family—how fortunate you have been. Why don't you tell the world about your wonderful marriage, your lengthy romance and fascinating life with Danny?" For us nothing ever got stale-but bread!

While reflecting back when I met Danny, it was like a slide show in my mind. It began with Danny the florist; cost accountant promoted to supervising accountant for Trailmobil; Northern Division Comptroller for Blue Chip Stamp Company; Vice President and Chief Financial Officer for Nob Hill Foods. Between his jobs at Blue Chip Stamp and Nob Hill Foods, I went to work to help out financially, getting a job behind a retail jewelry counter. He had a tough time for several years finding the right position with the right salary. I used to look for jobs in his field in the Wall Street Journal and then type all his resumes after I got home from work. Whew, how I remember those dark days! Tough stuff, yes, but we got through it together. I gave him encouragement and the support he needed, just as he gave me the strength and positive thoughts for my business ventures, helping me to become a successful entrepreneur with my own watch and clock business. We have all had the ruts and bumps in the road; getting over them-that's the trick!

Some other difficult times were when we had to cancel a tennis trip to Hawaii with friends because I needed an immediate hysterectomy. You know . . . that operation when they take out the crib, and leave the playpen! He was so sweet and attentive to me. Then I thought how he accompanied me to the surgeon's office to hear the blood curdling news that I had breast cancer. The doctor told us I would have to make a decision about breast surgery. After much deep thinking and talking about it, after a Mediterranean cruise and a land trip through Italy, with Danny's help and support, we decided to have a double mastectomy. That was the only way for us to have peace of mind. I have to tell you my husband was so adoring and wonderful while I was recovering. If you read my first book you would know Danny was a "boob" man and I was quite voluptuous. I always teased him about marrying me for my curvaceous body. Thinking back, the times I leaned on him were countless. Of course, I did the same for him. We gave each other strength. That was what made our marriage so wonderful. For an oldster, I am very adept and computer literate. Who taught me? Danny, of course! He taught me lots of things!

As I opened my eyes, the computer was ready to work. My fingers were on the keyboard and all of a sudden I was recalling so much from when I began working. My experience in retail, wholesale, as a factory rep, how I started my own watch and clock business, world travel, the international watch fairs over-seas, the several clubs we belonged to and how life was so great. I put it all in the computer for my book, entitled "Ya Wanna Watch? I'll Let Ya!" At the age of 80, I became an author.

Just a few pages . . . Danny's last stages
I told Danny what I was doing, showing him, with a new kind of excitement, a few pages of my book that I was writing. He read a little paragraph and he laughed. He laughed, that's all I cared about then. Something I wrote made Danny laugh! Now I had something to occupy my mind. I was totally blown away by the instant recall I had of way back at my first jewelry job as a sales girl for Besco Jewelers in Walnut Creek. As I placed the letters on the screen of my computer, I was amazed how I could remember every detail, every person and all the events that took place. That was way back in 1961.

Back to reality
Danny's painful gout was only getting worse, and he could not walk. He had to crawl to the table to sit down and eat his meals. He was not eating very much, but he was drinking a lot of cherry juice. Remember someone told me that it really helped get rid of the pain from gout? Well, it didn't help him. Thanksgiving was upon us and Rhonda, our youngest daughter, and her two children, Christopher and Courtney, were always with us. It was so heartbreaking for me, to watch

as Danny tried to crawl to the dining room table, before the kids arrived. He just couldn't make it! Turkey, stuffing, vegetables, Jell-O mold, cranberries, mashed potatoes, and vegetables filled the table. I tried to help him, but Danny could not make it. He crawled back to his bed, where he remained. We were all feeling so sad for him and ourselves, too. He ate nothing on Thanksgiving. It was the first and only time in our lives together that Danny did not sit at the head of the table on Thanksgiving! The reality of how dire his health situation was certainly now weighing in on all of us.

I continued to sleep in our bed, but it was difficult to get any sleep. He was constantly getting out of bed and crawling to the bathroom. I had to help him. It was getting too much for me to get him on the toilet. I decided one morning at 2:30 a.m., to give in and call the visiting nurse's phone number. I remember crying to her on the phone, "I can't do this! I don't know how to help him! Please, can you help me?" I have always been a person who does not like to ask anyone for help, as I've always been extremely independent. The following day the nurse came and checked Danny's vitals: pulse, blood pressure, heart rate, and the works. She suggested I call Hospice. I did just that and they were wonderful. They were such terrific human beings. I had never met such warm, caring people before. They had such inner strength; they were exceptionally comforting to me. I certainly admired them. They came and took over completely. There was a head nurse, Mike, who was the manager of the team, a young chaplain, who was great to talk to through my tears, a social-worker; also an occupational therapist, and of course, every day a visiting nurse came. It was heart wrenching to watch the deterioration of Danny, but there was no need to place Danny in the hospital. We all, including Dr. Joseph Kraut, Jr., our warm and comforting internist, agreed the best place for him was home in his own bed. For the next several weeks I engaged

Renette's Story

practical nurses from a home nursing firm in Monterey. Each had a 12-hour shift, so someone was here around the clock.

The morning of Wednesday, December 19, my dear friend Dawn called and said she and I were going to Monterey to look around Macy's, just to get away from the tragic scene I was living in. We stayed at Macy's for a while, but I was antsy, so we then went to lunch. After we ate, we drove home. I had a strange premonition all the way to Hollister. I had my cell phone with me, but I hadn't turned it on! As we drove into the driveway, I was surprised to see my daughter Rhonda, who came out of the house, to tell us that Danny passed away. They tried to reach me but could not get hold of me, so they called Rhonda. Dawn, Rhonda and I cried and hugged each other for the longest time standing in the middle of the driveway. Then my neighbor, Julie, came out, and we all hugged and cried some more. There are no words at times like this, just hugs and tears. Rhonda said she kissed her Dad goodbye. That was the saddest, hardest day of my life and, I'm sure, Rhonda's too. The realization didn't really set in for many days after that I would no longer see my sweet husband again. I went and stayed with Rhonda for one or two days. I cannot remember.

I did something very unusual, I guess. I emailed everyone in my computer address book letting them know what had happened. Mostly everyone already knew Danny was not doing well and they were always asking me for updates to his condition. Heartfelt sympathies came back via the Internet. A sad time! A very sad time! Then the phone calls and tons of sympathy cards came, but that finally stopped. My email address book, by the way, had 250 names. Many of the names were people we met on our trips around the world.

Coming back to the living, there was a lot to take care of. I was fully and solely in charge. Life goes on, and so do the bills. Thank God I paid the bills until Danny retired, when he took over the checkbook and bank statements. That was his thing. I knew everything about our finances, everything about our investments, so that was good. The difficult scenario was living alone. I have always been a people person and being with Danny for almost 56 years made it hard for me. Eating alone, sleeping alone, grocery shopping for one—I had to re-group, as they say. How, I didn't know at the time. Life changes, but it does go on!

Rhonda, our youngest daughter, was so caring, so supportive, and a huge help to me. Cathy, our oldest daughter, lives nine hours away. She called me often. Christopher and Courtney loved their grandpa, and they too gave me a lot of support and loving comfort. My large number of friends were equally sympathetic and wonderful to me. It's such a hard time, hard to know what to say and talk about. They all were great to me. The strange thing was that my son never came down to see me, never called to find out how I was doing, if I needed anything, or communicated with me in any personal way. No one from Danny's family called me on the phone, either, after the initial call of condolences the day after Danny died, but nothing since then. Very strange, I thought. It convinced me they just didn't care. It is more than four years since Danny's death with no telephone or personal email other than a couple of notes from one sister-in-law, and a couple of nieces, but that's all. It made me angry at first. However, the people from Hospice told me that's a very common reality among families. How sad that seems. Slowly I have learned to accept the things I cannot change, and have just gone forward. May God bless them all, anyway?!

Clothes to close
A most difficult task for me to do was going through Danny's closet, a month after he was gone, seeing all his beautiful clothes hanging there. He had such good taste and looked

so handsome in all the things he wore. It was time to clear out his stuff—his shoes, his suits, sports slacks and jackets, sweaters, and everything else he put on his body. I could still smell his scent. Where or to whom should I give his gorgeous wardrobe to? I called Hollister Community Services. They told me they give to people who need clothing, needy people who are honestly out there looking for work, but don't have the money to buy new clothes. Even his tuxedo, and dressy vests and cummerbunds were to be given to some person needing clothing. All in all there were ten large lawn bags filled to the brim with all of his personal wardrobe, all his shaving and personal toiletries. He wore Giorgio and smelled so good. I confess, I kept one new deodorant stick and one bottle of his aftershave. Once in awhile, I'll smell him! Silly, but his scent was always so sexy to me.

The end of January, I decided to reconcile the bank account. I used Danny's adding machine on his desk. I finished the task, balanced the checkbook, and put it away. I went over to my desktop computer to play one of my word games, great for the brain. All of a sudden I heard Danny's adding machine, like he was hitting the keys. I turned around and thought maybe I was hearing things. It was weird because it happened again, three more times. I looked to see if the plug was loose, but no, it was securely plugged in. Then I thought maybe we had a power outage, which frequently happens here at Ridgemark. I checked my microwave oven clock, a tell-tale sign, but it was okay, it had the correct time. Guess no power problem. I came back to play my word game. I heard nothing more from Danny's adding machine.

People had told me about strange events happening to people after a death occurs, but I was not a believer at all. A funny thing though, one day I went into the bathroom near the office and the toilet paper was upside down, like a left-handed person put it on the roll. Danny was left-handed. He would place the roll coming down under, while usually right handed people put the roll so the sheets go over the top. Hmm, that's strange, I thought, maybe it was my housekeeper. Peggy was there, so I asked her which way she placed the T.P. roll on the holder. She told me, "Exactly like you, over the top. Why do you ask?" I went into the bathroom near the family room, which Danny frequented a lot, while he was watching TV. Guess what? Yep, that roll too, was upside down, like a lefty would do. Quite strange that two bathrooms out of three had under rather than over the top! My bedroom bath was over the top.

One day, not long after the toilet paper episode, Rhonda had a very bad case of the flu, and bronchitis, close to something worse. I made some good old-fashioned Jewish Chicken noodle soup and took it the 45 miles to her home in Capitola, near Santa Cruz. She was sick. I took a bowl upstairs to her bedroom. She asked me to go to the market for her as she needed some groceries. I got her list and Courtney and I got in the car and drove to the store. We had fun, Courtney and I, shopping for her mom. After shopping, we checked out and when we got to my car in the parking lot clicked the trunk button and it opened. After putting the bags in and securing the trunk, I proceeded to click my unlock button on my keypad, and another strange thing happened. My seat, the #1 person's position, moved back to the #2 position, which was Danny's. I was number 1, and he was number 2. He hardly ever drove my Cadillac El Dorado. This developed to be a long fifteen minute session. Courtney kept saying, "Grandma, what's going on? Why is this happening?" The seat continued to move back to his position. I said "Courtney, I think your grandpa is playing games with us." I almost felt his presence, strange, but true! She was frightened, so I tried to make her laugh. But it was eerie, for both of us!

Renette's Story

Courtney's Grandpa and Grandpa's Courtney
Courtney always loved being with her Grandpa and vice versa. From the time she was a little girl to the present, she has always believed and said, "My grandpa is the smartest man in the world. He can answer any question I ask him!" Today at 19, her first year in college at Cal Poly, she has decided to follow her Grandpa's vocation which is finance/accounting. She is extremely smart. A woman in that field can travel far up the ladder plus the compensation is huge. Her Grandpa, I am certain, is so proud of her, as I am. At the end of this chapter you will feel the love, warmth and adoration from an essay Courtney wrote about her Grandpa. I read it, I cried, I loved it.

Author, author!
The manuscript for my book entitled "Ya Wanna Watch? I'll Let Ya" was finished after two years, and ready to send to a publisher. I had no publishers in mind because I didn't know of any. I was new to the book business. One afternoon after playing golf and having lunch with the girls at the club, I went outside on our deck. I was feeling kind of down. I looked up at the blue sky with a few puffy white clouds and yelled, "Danny, you're up there with the Big Guy, could you find out from him which publisher I should use for my book?" I didn't get an answer right away, but the next morning I went into the office, raised the blinds, looked at Danny's laptop on this little computer table and noticed an Entrepreneur magazine I had bought several weeks prior. I had never looked at it, so I opened the cover page to see staring me in the face an ad for InstantPublisher.com. There was my answer to the question of finding a publisher for my book. Can you believe it? Am I a believer? Yep, I am now! I certainly never was before, but I feel Danny's presence near me a lot of the time. Each morning I go into the family room and say, "Good morning, my darling," to a life size photograph that Rhonda gave me of her dad. I talk to him as though he is still actually here. My dog looks at me

strangely, but I still talk to the picture. I say, "Good night," to it as well. It's a photo that no matter what position in the room I am looking from, his eyes are always looking and smiling at me. His eyes follow me.

New knee—new pup pee
It was the latter part of February when I was playing golf with my friends, and on the sixteenth fairway my right knee collapsed. Poor Doreen had to help me back to the golf cart. I was in agony. My knee was so painful that I called an orthopedic surgeon recommended by my internist. He saw me the very next day and told me he thought I was a candidate for a new knee. We tried a cortisone shot, but it did nothing. It was obvious I needed knee replacement surgery. Swell, I thought, how am I going to do this? Danny is not here to help me. I talked to my doctor and he said he would arrange everything, and he sure did! The plan was to have the surgery on the 12th of March and stay in the hospital nine days when Rhonda would come and pick me up and stay with me until she had to go back to her teaching job after the Easter vacation. Cathy would then come down from northern California and stay with me for as long as I would need her. It was set, the surgery went well, and Taisun, our little black & white Shih Tzu, stayed at Rhonda's during my hospital stay. I came home with Rhonda, and all was under control. I went to physical therapy and progressed quite well. Rhonda left, Cathy arrived and things were going along well, but we noticed my little Taisun was not doing well, so Cathy said she would take him to the vet. Taisun never came back. The vet said he was mourning for Danny so deeply that he had a stroke. No husband, no dog and a new knee. After Cathy left to go back north to Bridgeville, California, nine hours away, I became lonely. I had never been without a dog my entire life, but I knew how much work it is having a new puppy. I still wasn't playing golf. I was just trying to adjust to my new knee.

Another friend of mine, Barbara Matulich, told me she was picking me up and taking me to see some puppies. How can anyone NOT give in to buying a puppy when he was such a fluffy, pearl gray, cute, furry, sweet little thing? Barbara drove me back to get my checkbook and I paid for my new little resident that I would raise. He was born on March 8, just four days prior to my knee surgery. What shall I name him? This was the end of April and I was going up to see my oldest and dearest friend, Louise, who has been my friend since we were both 11. Louise had been diagnosed with cancer and was being treated with chemotherapy. Louise loved Chinese food, so I told her I would bring our dinner—wonton soup and Chinese chicken salad, the very best this side of Hong Kong!

I told her that I bought a new dog and was going to bring him up to meet her and Monty, her pooch. I asked her to think of a cute name, and told her I was giving her the honor of naming him. She thought "Bogie" would be good. She loved Humphrey Bogart, and she asked me, "Doesn't that mean something in golf?" I told her yes, it's one over par, not spelled the same, but I didn't care. It made her feel good to give Bogie a name. My longtime friend just passed away a few months ago also. Thinking of my oldest friend allows me to talk about several early-on school friends, actually about 16 or so, all from San Francisco. We try to meet every three-to-four months for lunch at some restaurant close to the city. We all live in the Greater Bay Area, and we still have a great time enjoying each other—just guys and gals who grew up together. Hanging on to lasting friendships brings back such fun memories. We are now planning our 65th reunion for 2012. They asked me to be the emcee again. I did it for the 50th, 55th and the 60th. I guess I'm the only one who likes to talk. We all have had our share of illnesses and losses of a spouse, but we just hang in there and look forward to our food and fun lunch times together.

Merry Christmas—Oh yeah!
It was funny one day, lunching with the girls after golf at San Juan Oaks Golf Club, we were discussing this book, the one you are reading now, which had just gotten started, and something reminded Sue and I of one Christmas Eve when Sue and Mike hosted a dinner party for four couples. Mike went over to see his mom, and did not return for a very long time. We all seemed to be having a good time, but dinner was not served until after 9:00. By that time Danny and George had been drinking up a storm. We sat down at the dinner table and Danny was so stoned his face fell down onto his plate holding a beautiful slice of prime rib, potatoes, and vegetables. It was not funny then, but as I look back, I have to laugh. Imagine his entire face resting on his meal. I got George to help me take him home and put him into bed. I told you, Danny loved his cocktails!

Life goes on after death, so after self-publishing my first book, several boxes of them were finally delivered to me. The cover looked great, the printing was terrific, the six color page inserts looked very professional, and the back cover held the synopsis of what the book was about. Now it was time for me to get back to work. I wanted to see if I still had the selling skills and ability that abounded in me before, when I had my watch business.

I decided to start selling my book to bookstores. It really is a tough business, particularly in today's market. The first year I was very successful in selling as well as doing many book signing events. I sold at several Border's, a few independent book stores, as well as the Steinbeck Museum in Salinas. I did a book faire in Los Banos, several speaking events and was again on the road, loving the feeling of selling again. The book business is different from the watch business, but sales and marketing are the same, no matter what the merchandise. I'm still marketing my book, and getting my own press, but today it seems "ya gotta have a gimmick." I thought a good idea was for every book sale I made, the buyer could choose one of my designer quartz watches free. That is what I've been doing, and it's working! Are you asking why am I doing this? It keeps my brain busy. It allows me to be with all different kinds of people. I love meeting people and making new friends. When I sell my book and make money for another person's business, it makes me happy. A free watch given to the customer makes them happy. Everyone gets happy!

Bouncing back—going forward
I bounce around quite a bit—the reason is this is a serious book, but in my view, the reader needs to chuckle in between the heavy stuff.

Remember I told you about giving so many lawn bags of Danny's clothes to the community services? I didn't finish telling you the good thing was I could now utilize every closet in the house! All of my clothes are hanging so tightly in the closet that they are being pressed as I write this.

Rice everywhere & it wasn't even a wedding!
Someone after golf the other day talked about a new recipe for rice. That made me think of what happened one night when we lived in Lafayette. I made rice for dinner and to my surprise it didn't get cooked so I threw it down the garbage disposal. OMG, don't ever do that! Talk about surprise . . . when I came home that evening from playing Mah Jong with friends in Moraga, Danny and our son, Kenny, were baling out the washing machine. Yep, full of rice, and so was the dishwasher, bathtubs and one shower! I'm relating this to you because we all need funny things to reflect on after our husbands leave us. He was not happy—in fact, he was furious. We all laughed about it the next day, and I'm still laughing at it now!

A hole in my heart!
It's not an easy time, believe me . . . being a widow is tough. Sometimes waves of loneliness sweep over me, my eyes filling with tears. When this happens, I immediately go on to brighter thoughts, like reading my email, playing a word game on the computer, or playing with my dog. He always brings a smile to my face because he is so funny, so wildly crazy running around our orchard. He alters my sad mood to laughter. People have asked me about meeting other guys, I must confess, there is still so much love in my heart for Danny, there is no room for any other man in my life in that particular way. There are several men, who I associate with for business, and I have occasionally had lunch or dinner with them, but it's strictly friendship and conversation.

Going forward means you remember all the funny things, the loving things your husband left you with. That is a part of bouncing back. There is a serious side of what is left for you after you are left alone. I have been a widow for just four years and three months as I write this. It didn't take me that long, however, to figure out I had to take care of all the bills, the bank account, our investments, and repairs and replacements (such as if the water heater goes out). I never thought about any of these things before. I'm in charge now, so these things are a concern. I don't know much about carpentry work, but I'm learning to hammer nails in loose fence boards. I never had to change a light bulb. Danny did it! I now can unplug the kitchen sink with a plunger! Never ever did I put gas in my car! I have to do it because Danny is not here to do it for me. A dumb thing happened with my TV remote one day when I was not feeling well; it fell into a cup of hot tea (I think I fell asleep). Spilling it woke me up—I learned I am not good at programming a new TV control.

Danny taught me to save all receipts. I check all my monthly receipts against the various charges I made the previous month. There is a summary of charges on all your statements you need to reconcile with. I don't like it, but I have to do it. Make sure all your charge account statements coincide with your records, which you should be keeping. Are you? Watch for little charges like twenty cents or even less, on your phone bills, credit card, electric statements etc. Most people say it's too much trouble to check it out. I do. You can call the 800 number and ask what the specific charge is for. Be aware even computerized bills can be wrong.

Rhonda (so much like her Dad) got me into electronic banking. It's so easy, and a breeze to check your bank balance on your computer. I only pay three people by check now: my housekeeper, my gardener, and the pest control. I now take my car to be serviced to a very reliable auto maintenance and repair service, in whom I trust completely. Get yourself a good handyman to do some things you cannot do around your house. Know what insurance you have: auto, home, and life. Get a trustworthy accountant as well as a good attorney, whom you will need to change things over to you legally. Know your investments. Do you own your house? Where is the deed? Do you know? Know your financial status. This is crucial. This is your life!

I must tell you what happened a few weeks ago, and it's no joke! I just insisted that you check all your credit card and charge receipts. Well, I just got zapped by a company in Florida. This is unbelievable. Danny always said, "If you want to make money, you have to spend money!" At times, I do some goofy things that not too many others would even think of doing! I decided to send 25 of my books to one of the large news network TV stations in New York. I emailed each one of the TV newscasters that I was sending them my book as a gift. I was informed that I was the millionth person to email this particular network, so I was entitled to a "free gift." It would only cost the shipping charge of $3.95. My next credit card bill had a charge on it for, not only the $3.95, but another charge of $74.95 for a product I did not order, or want. It was some type of non-aging facial cream. It has become a nightmare trying to explain my dispute to the credit card company, with a gazillion telephone calls trying to make them understand I did not order this. I finally gave up and sent them a letter explaining the circumstances, which went out by US mail today. Again, I implore you to be very careful and scrutinize your bills.

Look at the bright side of things—just think, girl, you now have total control over everything in your life which you didn't have before. You are in complete charge.

A catalog of memories
I never stop thinking of Danny with his cool, calm and collected personality, which brings to mind one of our overseas trips to Germany. We were with a group seated at a table for 20 enjoying lunch, Danny at one end, a very heavy set man at the other. While eating our lunch we chatted with light conversation, never noticing the man at the opposite end of the table who was in trouble. Quick-thinking Danny bolted out of his chair and rushed to the man gasping for air, turning blue from choking on a large piece of meat. Danny quickly performed the Heimlich procedure actually saving his life!

Because of Danny
How and when I met Ava Marie was totally un-real. One day after Danny's death I received a phone call from Pat Riley, a real estate broker who was doing some sort of survey for the census bureau about staying in your home after someone died. I told her she would be welcome in my home, and I would be happy to answer her questions. She came in and we sat at the dining room table. For perhaps two hours we just sat and talked. I found her to be a delightful woman, and it seemed our personalities meshed perfectly. One day, quite awhile after

Renette's Story

I first met Pat, I got a call from her saying, "Renette, I would like to introduce someone to you. I think you would be perfect for her!" I had no clue as to what she was talking about, but I would soon find out. A young woman got on the other end of the line and asked me if she could come to my house in the next few minutes to talk to me. Quite puzzled, but interested, I said it would be fine. Ava Marie is a professional television interviewer. She explained the person she had planned to have on her show was unable to come, so after three hours of finding out about me, she asked if she could interview me the following Sunday. She learned through Pat that I had started up my own watch and clock company and that I was a successful entrepreneur. She also found out my husband passed away and I wrote and published my book, "Ya Wanna Watch? I'll Let Ya!" She was very impressed with me and my upbeat, humorous, and positive attitude.

We did the interview, which encompassed my unusual watch and clock designs, how I got into my own business by a fluke, sales and marketing, becoming an author, being a breast cancer survivor, and going through a lawsuit, and of course losing my husband. Ava and I are now very close friends. We talk on the phone often and meet each other for lunch or dinner as often as we can. If you want to meet my new young friend and see the interview, which turned out great, please go to Google/YouTube and type in "Spiral Up with Ava Marie—Renette Torres-Part I and Part II." It is only 20 short minutes. Watch it—you'll love it!

A collaborative effort to help you
The reason we wanted to compile this book, as I said earlier, is to help other women who are now widows, recent or long term, and women who will be widows in the future. This is a chronicle of several widows' stories, NOT by just ONE author, with only ONE perspective, but nine authors plus we added helpful tips, hints and suggestions to get you through this

difficult time. We show you how to forge ahead and adjust to your new single life without your man. We are all extending our heartfelt thoughts to you with a warm stretched out hand to help. It's not a fun time but I'm certain when you read these illuminating personal stories by REAL women (not reel women), you will be inspired. These are ladies of all ages, and I thank them for their contribution.

My name is Renette Torres. I am an energetic 83 year old (most think I'm 60), I am a widow. I am an entrepreneur. I am an author. I play golf (I just had my first hole-in-one), I play bridge. I play word games on the computer; play Hearts but the computer cheats! I still lunch with guys and gals from high school days every three months or so. I watch videos of Danny from our trips around the world—this allows me to hear his voice again. I will forever love and miss my Danny. He was my EVERYTHING! Everyone asks me how I am doing and I always reply, "how do I look?" They say, "you look great!" That's exactly how I'm doing!"

Chapter 2

Courtney's Story

(Courtney is Renette's granddaughter.)

More than a memory
"Death leaves a heartache no one can heal; love leaves a memory no one can steal."

This quote, written anonymously, incessantly repeated, and still plays itself, in my mind after the death of my grandfather. I will never forget the day my mom told me; the words felt like infinite bullets, paralyzing me with confusion and intense heartache. My hands were clammy, my heart pounded loud, vibrating in my ears with an excruciating sound. Everything around me was suddenly a complete blur. I had never lost anyone close to me in my family before, so the feeling was one I never was forced to grasp. The death of a loved one is a powerful struggle and I certainly wasn't prepared to face the battlefield. The victory was far ahead, comprising peace of mind and achieving a new level of maturity.

The relationship I held with my grandpa was certainly different from the average grandparent and grandchild. My grandpa was my hero, my idol, my dear friend, and my mentor. From sitting on his lap while rubbing the soft hairs on his arms, to coming up with outrageous questions and listening to him provide an answer to everything I asked, I cherished every moment with him. I remember boasting to all my friends because I had the "smartest grandpa ever," assuring everyone he would win the million dollars if he were to be on the show "Who Wants to be a Millionaire." I would sit in awe watching his fingers move rapidly on his adding machine. We would play puzzle games on his laptop for hours on end. His sweet and comforting smell still tickles my nose today. He was a man of wisdom, strength, integrity, laughter, and love. The bond we shared was genuine and infrangible; the memories embedded are precious and indelible.

How is one supposed to learn the feeling of death and losing someone? It is a feeling, rather than a lesson. Therefore, no one can simply teach you the feeling; it must be something learned by experience. Because my grandpa was my first loved one I lost, I had never really thought much about this feeling. I always assumed death was tragic, but never truly comprehended its depth because I never had to. When my family was flooded with this adversity, we had no choice but to be strong and absorb the heartache because there was nothing we could do to change what had happened. However, this tactic was not easy for me. I could not accept the fact that I would never see his face again, that I would never feel his arms around me, and that I would never hear his voice. It seemed unreal. How could someone be there and then simply not be there? I truly felt trapped in a nightmare where I could not wake up. The tears weren't ceasing and the sorrows continued to build. I was confined in this event that left my mind confused and longing for answers. "It will get better." "He is in a better place." "Everything happens for a reason." These words from family and friends appeared meaningless. I felt as if no one could say anything that would make the pain fathomable.

Though the pain still prevailed, a few months after his death, my heart and soul ascertained a feeling they both had never seized before. I finally developed the strength to see the good in my grandpa's death. I spent moments recollecting on the days we spent together, rather than grieving on how we could never relive those days. I gained the selflessness to be happy that he resided in a much better place, rather than mourning over the fact I would never see his face again. I realized that the death of my grandfather ended his life, but it did not end our relationship and the everlasting memories. Thankfully, I had my family and friends by my side through this whole experience. They were such an unbelievable support system. We all suffered and grew together. I began appreciating life with a whole new outlook. My convictions transformed. The cliché saying of "living each day as if there is no tomorrow" actually became tangible rather than simply words to me. This event certainly altered my perspective on society as a whole. I have discerned that there is no true panacea to this immense grief; however, hurdles are inevitable in life. In turn, they make a person stronger. They make a person more resistant and aware of the impediments we are forced to undergo.

Obviously I am saddened that my grandfather is not here to see my accomplishments in life. I wish more than anything he could walk me down the aisle on my wedding day, or live to meet my children, or see how I am following in his footsteps with my love for numbers and passion for accounting. Nevertheless, I know in my heart that he would be proud of me, and knowing that makes me so delighted. I owe a lot of who I am to him. Being such an admirable man, I know I am not the only one he affected throughout his life. His successes stimulated his recognition as a very notable and honorable man. Melancholy surely kindled amongst everyone he knew after his death. Reminiscing on the past undoubtedly fuels some of the pain that lingers with me, but those reflections make me feel exceptionally blessed to have shared such a special relationship with my grandpa and to be related to someone so virtuous. I will never stop missing him, yet I will never stop remembering him either. Like I said, death is a powerful thing. The battle is extensive and grueling; no one is ever prepared to face it. Nonetheless, it is our duty to live with no regrets and to focus on the things that truly matter because when a person is gone there is no way of getting any of it back. We cannot ignore death and its sorrows, but we can indubitably pay more attention to life and cherish every breath we breathe. Have I then conquered the battle? No, I do not think so, because the battle is never-ending. We are always going to be hit with new attacks, but I definitely am ready and willing to encounter whatever is thrown at me because of the lesson I have learned through losing my beloved grandpa.

Chapter 3

Lynn's Story

I was 25 when I met my husband, Ken, in 1976 at a restaurant in Palo Alto. He was tall, blonde, in good shape and incredibly handsome. He was also only 23, but told me he was 25 in hopes that I would give him the time of day. As it turns out, thank goodness, he told this "harmless" lie, as his assumption—that I wouldn't give a 23-year-old a chance—was right. As I learned more about Ken, I had a sneaking suspicion that he wasn't as old as he said he was. All of his friends were 23, he had only just graduated from university, but insisted he went straight from high school to university (that was back when people were able to graduate from college in four years), and he had a youthful look for a 25-year-old. About one month into our relationship, Ken forgot his wallet at my house. I felt guilty for my desire to take a peek inside to see whether he was really 25. My mom was there at the time and said, "What are you, crazy? Of course you should look in his wallet!" That's my mom. Sure enough, I opened up his wallet, looked at his driver's license and saw that he was 23-years-old. But it was too late—he had me hooked, so I didn't care about his age.

Our first date entailed a competitive game of tennis, swimming at the house where I lived in Menlo Park, and steamed clams and French bread at the Dutch Goose, still a popular restaurant today. At the end of our date, we kissed goodbye. Funny how this just seems like it was yesterday. Shortly after our first date, I went to Austria with my ski club. During the three weeks I was gone, Ken went to an insurance adjuster school in Seattle with Safeco Insurance Company. When I returned from the trip to the San Francisco Airport, I found my tall, sweet, handsome Norwegian man waiting for me at the gate. The wedding bells rang at San Mateo's Hope Lutheran Church in August 1978.

We purchased our first home in Moss Beach, about six miles north of Half Moon Bay. I worked in Palo Alto and Ken worked in the Financial District in San Francisco. We often met in the city and enjoyed going to restaurants and theatre with friends and coworkers. I became pregnant and had my first baby girl, Krista, at Stanford Hospital in 1980. I was 29 years old, one of the younger moms to have a baby at Stanford. We soon moved to San Jose, near Campbell, where Ken managed an insurance adjusting company. In 1985 my second daughter, Kari, was born at Los Gatos Hospital, California. This time, I was one of the older moms, now 34 years of age. I felt blessed to have two beautiful, healthy daughters and a loving, devoted husband.

After six years of living in San Jose, we really missed coastal living. In April 1989, we bought a home in Santa Cruz. Then, just six months later, the destructive Loma Prieta earthquake hit Santa Cruz on October 17. I still remember wondering if the home we just purchased a few months earlier was going to fall down. Our home survived, thanks to the new construction, and only had superficial damage. Ken's life was incredibly busy with claims after the earthquake. We even had insurance adjusters staying in our home for months following the earthquake, settling claims all over Santa Cruz area.

Lynn's Story

We loved our new home and the fact that our daughters could walk to school. Kari and Krista were athletic—both played tennis and swam. We enjoyed skiing as a family on the weekends. The girls joined Junior Theatre and Children's Shakespeare Santa Cruz and were involved in many plays. We had a vacation home in Tahoe City and regularly skied at Squaw Valley, Alpine Meadows, and Homewood ski resorts. In the summer we played golf, hiked in the mountains, rode mountain bikes, and went swimming in Lake Tahoe or in Santa Cruz's Monterey Bay.

We usually did everything as a family. Ken and I were avid windsurfers during this time and often brought our children to windy beaches like Half Moon Bay, Coyote Point, Waddell Beach, San Juan Reservoir, and the Gorge up in Oregon on the Columbia River. We also built a home on Lake Tulloch with Ken's father and his two brothers—all contractors. We enjoyed water skiing on Lake Tulloch in the summer and snow skiing at Bear Valley in the winter. Ken's mother, Inga, loved to cross country ski and would often carry a tired child on her shoulders while skiing. We enjoyed skiing with Ken's brothers and their children as well.

Ken enjoyed vacationing in Norway. In 1989, we flew to Germany to pick up a new Mercedes for his parents. We drove on the Audubon, trying to keep the speedometer under 60 mph. Before we knew it, though, we were cruising at 125 miles per hour trying to keep up with traffic on this fast freeway. From Germany, we took a ferry to Norway to meet my in-laws, Willie and Inga, and our daughter Krista. They had arrived in Norway shortly before us. We continued our vacation for the next month, traveling to Oslo, Måløy, and to the Lofoten Islands. Kari stayed with my parents in California where she attended summer camp.

Our next vacation to Norway included Kari and Krista, as well as my brother Glen. While visiting our relatives in Lofoten, Kari was able to attend school with her cousin for a week. This was an amazing experience for her as she was in fourth grade and very shy. This experience forced her out of her timid shell a bit and got her to open up to the other kids who wanted to hear all about California.

While visiting the Lofoten Islands, we ate out one night at a restaurant where one of Ken's cousins ordered whale and sea lion meat . . . . Ken was used to whale meat from his time spent living in Norway, but Sea Lion?! I think our Norwegian friends and relatives were trying to shock us. Well, mission accomplished! The band performing at the restaurant played California Girls while everyone danced, knocking into each other.

From Lofoten, we took a boat to Bergen, stopping in Måløy for a few days to visit relatives. We went fishing with Ken's uncle and caught plenty of fish for dinner that night. Kari was upset to see the fish bleed, as she did not like seeing fish suffer. We spent time in the home where Inga, Ken's mother, grew up. Apparently, one Christmas during World War II, Inga's entire family was barricaded in the basement while the English occupied their home. They were being shot at by the Germans. There were bullet holes in the side building, which served as a reminder of the home's rich history.

May 28, 2000—Incline Village, Nevada

It was a sunny, beautiful day up in Incline Village, a community on Lake Tahoe. Ken (47-years-old), Kari (15-years-old), and I (48-years-old) first hit a bucket of golf balls at the driving range next door to the condo we had just purchased as a vacation home. We were wrapping up our stay and had enjoyed a wonderful dinner the night before. Ken and I celebrated our new home in the Lake Tahoe area with martinis—Kari

Lynn's Story

celebrated with a Shirley Temple. We talked about the ski season, playing golf, and Tahoe's beautiful beaches.

To prepare for the drive home, we loaded up our SUV, which was pulling a trailer we used to move furniture into our new condo. The trailer was now empty, but the SUV was packed with our ski and snowboard equipment that we brought home with us at the end of each winter season.

We pulled out of Incline Village, saying goodbye to Lake Tahoe, and headed toward the Sierra Foothills to visit my parents. It was my father's birthday and his sister, Alice, was visiting from Chicago. Kari and Ken were as excited as I to visit Lake Wildwood. We humorously dubbed it, "Wally World." This was a takeoff on Disneyland, a place surreally unlike its natural surroundings, and also of National Lampoon's Vacation—a Nilsen family classic movie that we all related to and greatly enjoyed). We sat around the table enjoying lunch and birthday cake in honor of my dad. My parents, both avid golfers, discussed golf with Kari, who was on the golf team at her local high school in Santa Cruz. I noticed my Aunt Alice, who in her 80s, was still beautiful, had almost no wrinkles, and still had a sweet smile. My dad had a striking resemblance to Alice. My mother was beaming with pride with her family around her. She was in her 70's but could pass for someone in their 50's. I was thinking how lucky to have been born into this youthful, active family.

After a nice lunch and birthday cake, we said our goodbyes and boarded our SUV to head back toward our home in Santa Cruz. It was Memorial Day weekend so we were happy to get on the road early to avoid heavy traffic. It seemed like an end to a perfect weekend. Kari looked so beautiful at fifteen. She wore no makeup and her nails were meticulously manicured from her prom the weekend before. I was daydreaming and thinking about our older daughter, Krista. She was in Santa

Barbara and had just finished her semester in college for the summer. We liked her boyfriend and hoped they were coming for a visit soon.

The crash

I don't remember much about the actual accident. I felt our car begin to spin out of control, and Ken said, "Oh shit." In that moment, I knew we were in trouble, so I closed my eyes and pretended to fall. I told myself that I was falling down skiing; I relaxed my body and allowed myself to go with the movement and chaos all around me.

When I opened my eyes, it was hard to see. Everything around me was blurry. I could see Kari's hand laying limp under my hand. I saw her beautifully manicured, pink nails—each nail with a tiny rhinestone—lay motionless. I couldn't see anything else. I didn't know if she was awake or hurt. I also could not see my husband. I felt as if I were in a tight, dark hole.

Then I heard someone talk to me. I could just barely see that he was a uniformed Highway Patrol Officer. He told me we were in an accident. I tried, but could not move. It was then that I noticed I was hanging upside down inside the car. I asked him, "How are my husband and daughter?" The officer said he didn't know, but then he asked me, "Do you believe in God?" I told him "yes," and he proceeded to pray with me until emergency crews arrived. From there, my memory is patchy. I remember an ambulance ride to the hospital and, from there, a helicopter ride to another hospital where they could better treat my swelling brain. Everything was a blur.

As I lay there in the ICU, finally, someone came to tell me that my husband and daughter had been killed instantly during the accident. I closed my eyes and saw Kari's beautiful nails. I asked myself, "How could she be gone?" I imagined

Ken's voice screaming out. I remember praying with the on-scene officer. How could this be happening—everything hurt—my tears, my heart, my body and my soul. I was unable to move my head; there was a hard plastic brace holding my neck. I could not cry because the pain of my broken ribs was excruciating. I could only cry in small gasps. I felt God holding me. As my body and heart ached, I wanted to close my eyes, let go, and be with Ken and Kari. I saw life and death next to each other, and I wanted to choose which way to go. Time seemed to stop. While in the hospital, my remaining daughter Krista (20-years-old) stayed with me. She comforted me, held my hand, as she remained strong and loving. She was there for me and I was there for her. My desire to let go and die, to cross over to be with Ken and Kari, slowly faded. Krista was at my side and I had to be there with her.

While I was in recovery at the hospital, I learned that the person responsible for the car crash was a 28-year-old male, Raymond Cordova, who was driving with a 12-year-old passenger in the vehicle—both Cordova and the young passenger were drinking beer and were heavily intoxicated. Witnesses spotted Cordova throwing 40 ounce beer bottles from his car window. In an attempt to aggressively weave in and out of traffic, he clipped the trailer we were pulling. This caused the trailer to jack-knife, flipping our car three times on Interstate 5 just outside of Stockton, California. Cordova's car also flipped several times. A motorist passing by tried to help Cordova and the boy out of their car. When the two emerged, they fled the scene and ran across the freeway into a nearby neighborhood. This drew the attention of residents, so the police were notified immediately of two suspicious males running through the neighborhood. Both Cordova and the young boy were later apprehended by local law enforcement. I couldn't believe we were the victims of a drunk driving crash. It was so senseless, so easily preventable and so surreal.

Memorials and funerals—Santa Cruz, CA—June, 2000
Kari's high school had a memorial for her when I was still in the hospital. I was told that hundreds of students—many of Kari's friends, as well as many who were saddened to lose such a young member of the community—attended the memorial. It was such a shock; a beautiful 15-year-old girl was gone.

Kari, unlike her sister, was quiet and somewhat shy. She seemed to know everyone, yet she was so mild mannered and soft-spoken. How could someone with this disposition also be so popular? But in Santa Cruz, everyone knows someone who knows someone . . . and so it goes on. Her teachers reached out and helped obtain a bench and a rock memorial on the Harbor High School campus for Kari and Ken that said, "They worked hard and played hard." Kari was also known for her peacekeeping skills, bringing together friends who were feuding and getting them to be friends again.

Just after I was released from the hospital, I attended my husband and daughter's double funeral. Family and friends worked to make the arrangements, allowing me to focus on my recovery. Krista and Ken's two brothers chose caskets made of simple pine. Ken originally wanted to be cremated, but no one could bear to burn Kari's body—especially because we never discussed what she wanted. She was only 15 years old, after all. I knew Ken would understand our reasons for choosing to bury him next to his daughter rather than cremate him and bury Kari. The simple design and structure of the caskets allowed friends and family to write messages on the natural wood with Sharpie markers. This was the funeral director's suggestion—he told us that the victims of the Columbine shooting the year before had caskets signed by the community, almost like a yearbook, which could be healing for many of the funeral attendees.

Lynn's Story

Just as the memorial at Kari's high school overflowed with concerned, shocked, and saddened students, the chapel also overflowed to the street. An audio system was set up so people outside the chapel could hear the service. In addition to the minister speaking, those at the funeral who knew Ken and Kari were invited to take the microphone and speak freely about their memories. Friends, relatives and community members, all who were shaken by this loss, stood at the microphone recounting their memories of my husband and daughter. They shared humorous stories, as well as their shock and disbelief that they were really gone. Even today, the memory of their funeral is surreal—like a dream.

Many people said, and I agree, that Kari was an angel and, whether I like it or not, her time had come. Ken went with her and they waited in heaven for his mother to join them. Inga, Ken's mother, had terminal ovarian cancer. She was waiting to die after a long battle and was in incredible pain. Amidst her pain from cancer and her anguish at the loss of her son and granddaughter, there she was at their funeral. I find solace in knowing they are together now, looking down at us and giving us support and prayers from above.

Sentencing

Cordova was sentenced to 25 years in prison. He had been in jail most of his life and, at the time of the crash, had only recently been released from San Quentin. Krista was able to speak during the sentencing, and let him know how he took her wonderful father and sister from us in a senseless and selfish manner. Krista asked to speak first to ensure that Cordova would really hear her words. After Krista spoke, several other friends stood up to speak at his sentencing to ensure the court truly understood the impact this loss had on our family, friends, and on our community as a whole.

At one point, Cordova made his statement in which he told the court that he only did what so many other people have done—he just got caught. While it was painful to hear this lack of accountability and outright denial of his actions that took the lives of two people, it was healing to hear the words of support from family members and community members who were impacted by the loss of Kari and Ken. People spoke about the qualities of Kari and Ken and to the incredible void left behind them. The court also scolded Cordova and made it clear that his lack of accountability was nothing short of disturbing. Even his grandmother, who attended the sentencing, approached me afterward to hug me and to apologize for her grandson's actions.

With the completion of the sentencing, I healed a little bit more. Healing, I have found, is a long process that is by no means linear or intuitive, nor is there a one-size-fits-all, quick-fix solution. Just when I think I'm doing great, the sentencing gets postponed, and I'm filled with a sense of dread, yet again, and anxious anticipation. Or I come across Kari's watch, reclaimed from the crash, with blood on it, and my stomach turns. Or I think again about Cordova and how his reckless behavior irreversibly changed the course of my family's life.

While the sentencing did not minimize the pain of Ken and Kari's death, its finality allowed me to heal. Leading up to the sentencing—over one year after the accident—was a seemingly endless stream of legal processes and court subpoena delays. If memory serves, the sentencing was delayed on three different occasions, which wreaked emotional havoc on all of us. To have the sentencing behind us all, to know Cordova's fate, to feel free to move forward, surprisingly, felt like a large weight lifted off of my shoulders.

Lynn's Story

Life after the crash

As I sit here today—nearly 12 years after losing my husband and daughter—I have reason to feel down at times, but there is more reason to be grateful. I suppose the best word to define this feeling is "bittersweet." Yes, I lost the love of my life and my beautiful, intelligent, kind-hearted daughter. Yet, I have an incredible surviving daughter for whom I am grateful every day to have in my life. And together, we have survived.

I also have an incredibly supportive network of friends and extended family around me who stepped up and helped my daughter and me tremendously. I often hear about families torn apart amidst loss and feel fortunate that ours was drawn so much closer together. We are truly blessed in spite of our past misfortunes.

Shortly after the crash, my friend Lolin approached me and asked whether I would be willing to help organize a golf tournament to commemorate Ken and Kari. Golf was a big part of our lives; Ken and I played often and Kari was on the high school golf team. Over the course of the year following the crash, a committed group of friends and members of the Santa Cruz golf community worked to organize the Kari and Ken Nilsen Golf Tournament. We held the tournament close to the first anniversary of Kari and Ken's death, which, in hindsight, was a healthy way to honor them.

The Kari and Ken Nilsen Golf Tournament raised more than $30,000, and provided several years worth of financial support to female, high school-aged, college-bound golfers, and to Santa Cruz Junior Golf, an organization with which both my daughters were involved as children. Santa Cruz Junior Golf developed the Kari Nilsen Golfer of the Year award that is still offered each year to a young, local golfer. This award is a plaque that hangs on the wall at Delaveaga Golf Course—it is heartwarming to see the community remember

Kari year after year. The Harbor High School Golf Team, Kari's team, also dedicated the 2000 season to Kari. I still have the team's 2000 uniform t-shirt. It is light yellow and says "Kari 2000."

One of Kari's high school teachers also arranged to have a tree planting ceremony and bench dedication at Harbor High School, where Kari attended school when she died. Today, there is a beautiful tree planted on the campus. Next to the tree is a bench where Kari's friends used to hang out at lunch time. There is also a boulder next to the tree and bench with a plaque that honors Kari and Ken.

Lolin, my friend who spearheaded the Kari and Ken Nilsen Golf Tournament, passed away just a few years later. As a way to remember both Lolin, Kari, and Ken, our families worked to get a bench in their names at our local yacht harbor, which is an area our family always enjoyed. Today I often go sit at this bench, dedicated to my friend and family, and enjoy a cup of coffee. It is a way for me to honor them, to remember them all, in a beautiful place they all enjoyed.

My husband provided for us through his life insurance. Thanks to his due diligence, I was able to invest in commercial property that provides me with a steady income. This has provided for my daughter's education and allowed me to keep our home. This also allowed me to keep our home near Lake Tahoe in Incline Village.

At the time of our loss, Hospice of Santa Cruz proved to be a wonderful resource and offered grief counseling. I asked our grief counselor how she knew the details of the crash and she told me she was at the high school providing counseling to students after Kari and Ken died. Two of my close friends were involved with Hospice as well, and due to their encouragement, my daughter and I attended bereavement support groups to share our story with others whose losses were more recent. In one instance, we attended a session for a family who lost a child suddenly and very similarly to how Kari and Ken died. It was difficult to witness the pain we knew so well, yet it became healing to help others. We knew that both time and support from family and friends were important in recovering from such an incredible loss. Communicating about our loss helped us in moving through the first year. It felt good to be able to share this advice with a family who was in the throes of their more recent loss, to be able to show them that there is hope ahead, and that it will not always be so tremendously sad, but they will actually enjoy life again one day.

My daily walks were therapeutic. Sports were our family's mantra; from golfing and skiing to biking and swimming, staying active was more important than ever.

My daughter took off a few semesters from school and I was worried she would not finish her education. She worked at Heavenly Valley for a few ski seasons and this seemed to push back her education substantially. She always assured me she would finish school, knowing this would have meant a lot to her father as well as me.

In June, 2011 Krista was hooded, receiving her masters degree in Communication Studies at San Jose State University. She lived with me during graduate school and worked to support herself through school. She recently joined a high tech company in Silicon Valley, working in employee communications. She married a wonderful man, Michael, and they just had their first child, a baby boy named Beck William, three months ago. I know that Ken and Kari would not only approve of the path she's taken, but they would be very proud of Krista and Michael and all that they have accomplished since coming into each other's lives.

It has been nearly 12 years since the crash. Time moves on. I often think of Ken, my wonderful husband, and Kari, my beautiful angel. My grandson knows me as "Mormor," which is Norwegian for mother's mother. In part I chose this name to honor Ken and his strong connection to his Norwegian upbringing. It is a way to still feel as if he is a part of the grandparent experience with me.

I play plenty of golf these days. I'm the membership chairperson for the DeLaveaga's Women's Golf Club. I also belong to Pajaro Valley, Bayonet and Blackhorse, DelMonte, San Juan Oaks, and Incline Village Women's Golf Clubs. My daughter and I enjoy going stand up paddling in the Monterey Bay and also in Lake Wildwood. Sometimes her dog Maeby, a Rhodesian Ridgeback, rides on the board with her. Krista and I also continue to ski in Lake Tahoe each year.

There are days when I miss Kari and Ken so much it pains my heart. But I know they are always here around me, spiritually. I will always love Ken and Kari, just as I love Krista and those around me now. While it hurts to think about how life might have been with them still here, my heart warms at the thought of all the support our community put forth after their untimely death. In order to heal, I've found that I need to really feel the emotional pull and go through the pain of the loss. As I've heard my friends at Hospice say so many times, you have to go through it to get through it. Suppressing the feelings of sadness only makes things harder because they will manifest in one way or another. Over the past 12 years it has become clear that the true healing comes when I remember and honor Kari and Ken. Through all of these rituals—golf, daily walks, sipping coffee at the memorial bench, talking with other survivors—I move through the loss of Kari and Ken and learn to accept this loss.

Chapter 4

Shirley's Story

The Born Widow

Is it possible that one can be born a widow? I often think that it was predestined that I face the world alone. Is it nature or nurture that predicts our future? My earliest recollections are of being quiet, shy, and isolated from others. I can remember stories about how my brother threw a fit the day they brought me home, screaming, "take it back" There are pictures of him glaring in the background as I experienced my first birthday cake. My mother was always telling her friends what an easy baby I was . . . just put me down with a toy and I would sit for hours. What she didn't see was that those "quiet" times were often interrupted by my brother displaying his anger in hurtful ways. It seemed that my contentment triggered his upset. I learned early that there was not much support, that verbal abuse was the communication style, and that my mother wasn't prepared to defend us. My growth and safety was predicated on sidestepping the males in the family.

This was around 1949 in Fresno, California, when I was four years old and just starting school. I had been at home with a brother who didn't want me around, with a stay-at-home mom who didn't drive, and a father who was "on the road" working, and, as I later realized, doing a good bit of drinking. I don't know if no one spoke of it or if I didn't hear, but I swear

I didn't know I had to go to school until the day I was walked there and dropped off. The fear of being in unknown corners was so strong that I instantly stationed myself under the piano, trying to go unnoticed until I could figure out where I was and what I had to do. The first thing I couldn't do was the Pledge of Allegiance, the second was to tie a shoestring or make a bow. My Buster Brown buckle shoes were the best for starting kindergarten, but not so good for learning to tie shoes. When we accomplished this task, we got to pin a paper shoe bearing our name on the bulletin board. I think my little shoe was one of the last on the board, and I remember feeling shame and embarrassment. My later, modest success at being able to tie shoe laces paled when I was told I was too chubby to ride on the big turtle someone brought to the school. Quite possibly, I would have been more prepared to start school at five years of age, but I do believe those feelings of inadequacy were the seedlings of my motivation to learn and to take care of myself. I did not want to spend my life under someone else's piano.

During my school years, especially the years without television, I had no reference for normal. My home and my family were all that I knew. There were no girls to play with in the neighborhood, and the boys were outside being boys, so I found my life in books. My favorite day of the week was Library Day. I could return books, check out more, and when all else was chaos, get lost in the stories of other families and other kids. My all-time favorite was *The Boxcar Children*. This tale of orphaned children who stayed together in a boxcar at the dump was the ultimate survivors' story. It represented adventure, suspense and the happy-ever-after that we all used to expect. Many times I have thought of the effect that story had on me and I can almost say it saved my life. With no stable foundation in my home, I read and believed that I could take care of myself by being creative, assertive, and strong. I couldn't have verbalized this knowledge at the time, nor would I quickly use it. The influence and guidance that would normally come from real life was presented to me in literature.

A huge event occurred during my 8th year. Concurrently, my first best friend moved in down the block and we got a TV set. My world opened up so fast that I experienced culture shock for years. I lived in between two worlds, the one at home and the one we created through playing and dreaming and watching the Mickey Mouse Club. We set out on our bikes on a daily basis to conquer our demons, and in our minds, we succeeded. Two very shy personalities triggered a brat reaction that made us feel untouchable. Together, we could shed our layers of fear and strike out in search of adventure and fun. She was adjusting to a life with a new dad, while I was not adjusting to a life with alcoholism. Put us on our bikes, and the world opened wide. We were diminutive Doña Quixotes, chasing our windmills on our two wheeled donkeys! Mileage wise, we didn't get too far, but experientially, we zoomed, we darted, we fell, we got lost, but we never didn't get back on our bikes. They were our connection to the free world. Finally, a basis from which we could grow, and as we got older, we grew in different directions. No judgment, no criticism, just friends supporting friends. Her goal was to get married and be taken care of, my goal was to continue my education and to be on my own. She wanted to meet lots of boys, while I wasn't allowed to date. We graduated from riding our bikes to riding the bus, exploring farther from home as we remained rooted at home.

With no role models for male relationships, I bounced off of people, liking them, but not knowing how to relate. I loved the challenge of the chase, but had no idea what to do with what I caught. When I turned 19, I met a young man who was just out of the Navy, working for his dad. In high school, he hung out with the "Neat Street" kids. This designation was reserved for those with the right background and right address, north of our school. I was amazed that he liked me, since my neighborhood bordered on ghetto in the Fresno culture. Putting dreams of my future on hold, I let myself become part of a relationship. We did it all backwards—sex first, conversation second, and realization third. I was pregnant, devastated by my choices, and discovered that this man-child had no plans other than to live off of his dad. I had a part-time job in a hospital, and, at that time, an institution with a rule against working there while pregnant. When we tried to discuss finances and how we could manage, his solution was that we would buy a boat with my salary until I had to quit, and then let his dad pay for the baby. I argued that issue, he hit me, and that was it. I picked myself up off the floor, stunned that I had picked a man meaner than those at home. There was no marriage, no divorce, just the instant demise of an "almost" family. I was hurt and disappointed. The horror of having to take this problem home was no worse than the horror of ending up with the wrong person. I was like a widowed mother-to-be, on my own in an unfamiliar setting. Luckily, times were changing in the early sixties. My boss went to my defense and, for the first time in hospital history, I was allowed to keep my job while pregnant.

During this time, my father passed away, and my poor mother embarked on her widowhood by preparing for her first grandchild. My focus was on my job and becoming a parent. My experiences with family gave me the belief that a child with two miserable parents was not better off than a child with one responsible parent. At that time, there were no alternatives, and I have never questioned my decision to go it alone. Instinct told me that my normal was abnormal, and I had to learn to trust myself before I could trust others.

I was soon immersed in life learning and began to understand money, security, and responsibility. I was able to stay with my mother for a time, learning how to relate to her as an adult. In many ways, this baby was a gift who appeared in a troubled space. He brought instant joy where there had been darkness. He opened hearts that had started to shut down. I could step up and make smart choices with him as the inspiration. I realized that although I was not married, I would never be single again. Men my age were either in or dodging Vietnam and there was little common ground to build upon. It is difficult to be the mother and the father to a toddler, then turn into a hot date for three hours on Friday.

My son and I basically grew up together; my job led to a training program, which in turn led to a license and a career. We moved out and moved up, but still were only surviving. I saw an ad in the newspaper for a one-day seminar put on by a local financial planner. The featured speaker was Jean Shinoda Bolen, author of *The Goddess in Every Woman*. The deal was that you paid for the seminar and then got an hour of financial counseling in return. This was a life altering experience. We talked about money, we talked about women and money, and the gist of it all was that women are not comfortable having their own, so they don't let it work for them. In the late 1970's, ERA times, this was a novel idea. We were asked to list five roles that we played throughout the day, and I am sure, when it was done, I was not the only one who didn't have myself on the list. This *aha* moment brought me to tears. What a simple thought—make room for yourself! It is the first time I had permission to have wants and needs. I had spent time being a daughter, a mother, a co-worker, then boss, but I had not yet been me. How could I expect to find someone to share a life with if I didn't know who I was? I have always been grateful that I was so busy with work, parenting, and school during this time. My self-imposed widowhood saved me from a dozen divorces!

I did take advantage of the one-hour financial counseling, and was horrified when she asked me if I could try to save $10 a month! I made good money. I had bought my first house, and I had not one dime put away. She taught me to pay myself first, to take advantage of payroll deductions for pretax savings. She taught me to be both the husband and the dad! I went back to school, taking evening classes at San Jose State College. I got my first degree 20 years after I graduated from high school, and ten years later finished a graduate degree at Chapman College. I put a trip to Greece on my charge card and then spent three years paying for it, but my world, my dreams and my future opened up tenfold. I had a list of places to be and things to do that would keep me occupied for multiple life times, and always knew that settling down would not happen unless all this went with it. I promised myself I could trust my decisions, not have to go backwards, and know that being alone did not have to mean being lonely.

I took advantage of the insurance benefit to see a psychologist when I realized my son would be leaving home at some point and I would have to remember who I was when I was nineteen, before this major detour popped up. I wanted to understand more about myself, what made me who I was, how I could share it all with someone. I learned that there was a lot of damage, sorrow and anger. I realized that there was a lot of work to do in order to create a sense of peace and balance in my life. This begins to take place when the past is properly dealt with and the future is eagerly anticipated.

Adjusting to change is a shock to the system. Changes that bring grief, pain and upset are felt in every area of our being, and time should be given to the process that will bring healing. My tip for anyone who has to face a new challenge is to quietly be with your feelings. Let memories of the past remind you of what works and what doesn't. Incorporate that which works into your future, bless the other and let it go. It

Shirley's Story

is a good exercise of the heart and mind to get back to your beginnings. Who is your true self? What do you bring to the table and how would you like to build on that? They say that as children we knew who we were and what we wanted. Years of layering often cover up that innocent, instinctive perfection of mind and spirit. It's time to start a new bucket list . . . what have you always wanted to do, and what would you have done differently? What resources do you have available and how will you use them? Now is when we get to draw our own map and delineate our own route. It can be straight to an end, or it can meander. It can be a trip in the fast lane or a switchback that takes some time.

Your choice, your future.

You are much stronger than you imagine, you have unique experiences to bring to any new situation. There will be many forks in the road and you will be the decision-maker. Trust that you will take care of yourself and know that you can find your way back from any wacky adventure. This will be your time to discover how the world will work for you and where you want to fit in. It is important to be engaged in your life, to sign up rather than drop out. If you are embarking on a new course, actively set a direction. It's too easy to be brought into others lives, and a pitfall to live yours through them. A loss is never totally overcome, but, rather than let it drive you, let it help you steer.

I realize now, after a lifetime of contemplation and years of therapy, that odds were not great for me to pick a good mate. I often say that I have lived my life backwards. I was born old and will progressively get younger. I don't like extremes, so I am committed to finding a middle. I tend to have a clearer vision if I am seeing things from my center. I have gone to psychics, had my cards read . . . I have a video of my aura and, when I had my numbers done, was told I was on my last life, and totally evolved! I love whatever is next. I want challenge and adventure in my life, and I try not to have too many strings attached. Writing this chapter has been somewhat discomforting, due in the most part to the need to travel back in time and remember. I always learn something from revisiting the past, but also harbor a secret fear that if I go too far, I will not be able to come back. There is no happy-ever-after ending because the next chapter is still being written, but there can be peace. When I was younger, I switched between being the mom and the dad, the nurturer and the breadwinner . . . evolving the "me" who continues to learn, and strives to accept. Now I am in the sandwich generation, hovering somewhere between daughterhood and parenthood, wiping a different nose, and spending the bread I made.

I am ever grateful for my friends and extended family. They have laughed and cried with me. They have always ignored my bad judgment and applauded my successes. They are the pillars to lean on, and they will always balance the other end of the seesaw . . . sharing the weight, lifting me when I am down. We move along different routes, but always with an awareness of those who are special, always leaving the same message . . . take care, safe travels.

Chapter 5

Helma's Story

Looking back at my life, now 75 years in the making, I have to acknowledge my mom who *always* had my back, who *always* supported me in *whatever* my planned adventures would be, even when I told her that I was planning to leave the country of my birth behind.

For two years I had already experienced the city of London, and definitely "nixed" that part of Europe on my list of places for consideration of my chosen "homeland." It was now reduced to two places—Australia and the USA—and I do not need to tell you which land of the free won my heart. In my younger years, I was introduced to the occupational armed forces, including the Americans. It was love at sight of the American soldiers with their demeanor, and eventually I embraced their country's philosophy.

It was in late 1961, while working as a secretary for the American Armed Forces Civil Services in Frankfurt, Germany, that I, a German civilian, with the luck that so often followed me throughout my life, found in my hand a notice from the American Consulate. It informed me that a friend of an acquaintance of mine was ready to sponsor me in the United States, and enclosed were instructions for the final steps required in order to receive my visa for immigration to Tempe,

AZ. The deadline to complete all of this gave me barely four months to complete the necessary steps, plan, and pack.

It was on the 31st day of March 1962 that I arrived in San Francisco, and passed immigration, customs, etc. Waiting to welcome me was my former American boss, Rob. Rob was stationed in Heidelberg at the headquarters of the office to which I was assigned, approximately 90 miles south of my place of employment in Frankfurt. He and I had remained in touch after he completed his tour in Germany and was assigned to Maryland, and then later reassigned to Fort Ord, CA. Rob highly recommended that I make a stop in the Monterey area prior to completing my immigration to Arizona. Rather than bore you with details, let me just say—once I saw Carmel-by-the-Sea and the beach Rob took me to on the day of my arrival, I never left, never regretted it, and was happy that I made the snap decision to stay.

Although publicly separated from his wife, legally Rob was still married, and his then wife had moved from Maryland to Florida to be with her daughter. Not too long after my arrival, Rob and I began what would be our "common law marriage," living together for 21 years.

Rob retired from the US Army after 23 years of service and started working for the City of Pacific Grove, CA. He had found a job doing what he liked to do—working on vehicles. In this case, he was keeping the City vehicles in tip top running condition; in other words, he was their automotive technician. It was during that time that we tried our skills at amateur automobile racing.

I had bought a house in Pacific Grove, CA, with a big, beautiful backyard, and thus we had room enough for Jacques, my silver Poodle, and Sabrina, a black Labrador (definitely Rob's dog). We had wonderful times during those years.

Helma's Story

After living several years in Pacific Grove, Rob became ill. It started with just shoulder pain. "Arthritis" was the diagnosis back then—take some aspirin, and if that doesn't help, see the doctor again in two weeks. The pain did persist, getting stronger by the day. Our planned trip to Germany to visit my family was split up. On Rob's urging, he sent me on that trip alone (but he would go later for a visit); his pain was just too much for him to be sitting for 11+ hours in a plane. Off I went, but with mixed feelings. On my return, I discovered that Rob was much worse—his fingertips looked as though they were rotting (it was, in fact, gangrene) he could not walk and had to crawl to the bathroom. He could not even hold a fork and/or knife to eat. No physician was able to diagnose these symptoms and attribute it to any specific disease. In desperation, Rob even had a dentist pull all of his teeth, hoping that might be the source of some infection in his blood, but to no avail.

My wonderful boss, who had great connections, finally intervened, and he assisted in getting a referral appointment with a hematologist at Stanford Hospital in Palo Alto, CA. The instant diagnosis was that Rob had "Wegener's Granulomatosis." Wegener's is an uncommon type of inflammation of small arteries and veins (i.e., an incurable form of vasculitis). It classically involves inflammation of the arteries that supply blood to the tissues of the lungs, the nasal passages (sinuses), and the kidneys.

We wondered if Rob might have contracted this disease during his Vietnam tour in 1964-1965, but NOT SO according to the expert physicians at Stanford. Rob had to stay in the hospital, and I needed to get home to our canine "children," Sabrina and Jacco (short for Jacques), as well as my job.

Eventually, after medical treatments similar to those for cancer, Rob came home. We had sold our home in Pacific

Grove, bought property in Carmel Valley, CA, and were in the midst of building our "dream home." Unbeknownst to me, Rob had initiated his divorce, and invited my brother and sister-in-law to fly here from Germany to be witnesses to our quickly-arranged marriage in Reno.

Before long, we moved into our new home, pushing worries about Rob's illness aside. We were too busy getting things done the way we wanted—the landscaping, building fences and decks, etc.

It seems as though the legalization of our togetherness gradually corrupted our "bliss" and there were more and more unhappy days. I felt that Rob had become extremely possessive, and part of that was my fault for having allowed that situation to exist for so many years. I began to revolt, and tried to reassert my independence, while Rob had no clue what to make of my change. He too felt different, simply going to work, eating, sleeping, and then going to work again—a never-ending, unexciting routine for him. His response to my suggestions, such as, "Let's pack a suitcase and go off into the wild blue yonder for the weekend," was usually, "those things need to be planned."

One day the surprise came. Rob informed me that he was moving out because he was tired and he had enough of the miserable time we now experienced together. Honestly? I was relieved! I too was tired of the negativity surrounding us. We started to pack Rob's things for the new place that he had already rented.

In the meantime our Jacco had to be put down—age and complications with his teeth had made his life a hard one. To boot, Sabrina had developed violent seizures, but Rob and I both dealt with it.

Helma's Story

The treatments at Stanford had held Rob's disease in check. With every day that passed after the "Rob MAY live no more than six months" prediction, the threat of his "terminal illness" had paled, almost been forgotten. Now, seemingly out of nowhere, it flared up again wildly. Rob's plan to move out was no longer an option, and I refused to be the captain that left a sinking ship. Twice a week we drove to Stanford for blood transfusions until finally the local hospital agreed to provide the service.

Just before Christmas 1988, my niece Charly and I returned from a Christmas tree lighting ceremony, and found Rob in bed, and he was incoherent. We rushed him to the hospital where tests were taken, and biopsies performed. Finally they told me that he was misdiagnosed. He did not, as they explained earlier, suffer from pneumonia, but rather his now 9 ½-year-old blood disease had reared its ugly head again. On New Year's Day in 1989 Rob took his last breath. It was over, the suffering, the inevitable had arrived.

That evening, on my way home, tears ran down my cheeks, but I did not cry, somehow I felt numb, emotionless. What now? I had to push all of the questions back and hurry home to my dog that may or may not have had another seizure and needed my help. It hit me that I, on my own, had to take care of an epileptic dog, pay attention to my job, arrange Rob's final journey and, and, and . . . .

The next day I went to the funeral home and made arrangements, and my mom called to announce her arrival—to give me comfort and to see that I would not be so alone. She was 80-years-old, and spoke no English, but she tried to be as much help as she could. Little did the two of us know how much more intense and frequent Sabrina's epilepsy would become; Mom had no experience with dogs or any other domestic animals and she was frightened. Finally, three months after Rob's death, a veterinarian sent Sabrina off to join Rob.

New lessons started immediately. One of our solar panels had developed a strong condensed water drip, causing the accumulated water to penetrate into the house, under the foundation. I decided to take Rob's pickup (now actually mine) and go to a building supply store. When trying to explain to a salesperson what I needed in order to build a "French drain," I was interrupted with, "If you don't know what you need or want, I cannot help you," and I was left standing there. It hit me—I am not a MAN, so I am presumed not to have knowledge about a MAN's job! While sitting in the truck in the parking lot, I felt helpless, and I cried and cried—all that was bottled up finally came out.

After awhile, my courage came back, and I recalled Rob's words, "You can do it, just put your mind to it," and "go stand up for yourself." These were words he always said to me before I had to face the dreaded weekly department head meetings, with me being the only female. I marched back into the store, demanded to see the manager, and did not hesitate to point out his rude salesman. I then explained my dilemma with the solar panels. He apologized, knew what I needed, helped me out, and I left, feeling that I could face the world, even without Rob. That is, until I met one of Rob's fellow employees. His first words out of his mouth, before any consoling muttering, were, "Oh, I see you are driving ROB'S truck!" My blood started to boil—Rob's truck?! Rob was dead, and so I resolved that issue with my newly found independence by going straight to the DMV and asking for and receiving personalized license plates for MY pickup with HELMA as the plate number.

One little lesson after another gave me more and more self-confidence. I took charge of matters, dealing with roof-repair people, tree-trimmers, and yes, I even learned how to use a Rototiller in my backyard (dressed in a bikini and flip-flops)—a strange sight to my neighbors, I am sure. All this time, the Christmas gifts were still lying under the tree, never to be opened by Rob. His closet was still packed with his wardrobe, the garage full with his unbelievable assortment of tools, some dating back to our happy times when he was in amateur auto racing and let me be part of his pit-crew. Rob's best friend, Dick, came to pay me a visit. I gave him the gifts, most of the tools, and all of Rob's clothing. Dick had a similar build to Rob's and so it worked out well. Dick then sent by a tool-man who bought the remaining tools and the huge toolbox.

Slowly but surely, I was fine, had become stronger and learned to make decisions without him. I am convinced that Rob paid me a visit as a friendly ghost on one occasion. As I used to do while Rob was alive, I was sitting in the family room watching TV when I saw him coming down the hallway to check on me as he used to do to make sure I had not fallen asleep. I was not scared, and felt sure that he nodded his approval on how I had handled myself, including the decision to sell our rather large house. I found that I had confined my living to one bedroom with an attached bath, the family room and the kitchen, and had shunned the sunken living room, dining and sewing rooms, and the remaining two big bedrooms with two additional full-baths. There was a huge amount of landscaping to be kept up, decks galore to keep in shape, and with only me to do these chores. OK, Mr. Realtor, do your thing!

A year and a half later, still no house sale! One of the girls that worked for me asked me with a grin if I would be opposed to her setting up a blind date for me. Well, life has to go on, I thought—I should give it try. I met my date, and we hit it off right away. I was then 54-years-old, and I had often thought that Rob had left me not soon enough for a new chance at love, and too late to have some excitement in my life. At the beginning of this chapter, did I not mention I have always been very lucky in my life? Once again luck was by my side. My new man, Lance, was young (13 years my junior, to be exact), loved to laugh, and was ever-ready for the next adventure. He was full of life and quickly ready for all kinds of suggestions—"Let's do this or that"—on the spur of the moment. We loved the wild ride on a cigarette speed boat across the waters, parasailing in Hawaii, we enjoyed repelling in the Moaning Cavern (east of Stockton, CA), and loved sailing on his 54' Schooner. We started building our own catamaran that we wanted to move to Costa Rica after having vacationed there several times and loved that part of earth. We had a blast and savored every moment. Once again I felt so very much alive. BUT . . . .

Good things seem to always come to an end too soon. My new knight in shining armor suddenly lost a lot of weight and his skin seemed to have a yellowish tint. After all kinds of applied help (holistic medicine and such), the official diagnosis was pancreatic cancer. I watched his suffering as the life slowly drain out of Lance's body, and not even at 55 years-old, he too left me and this earth. It was not long after this that the house on top of the Carmel Valley's hills was sold and I moved into a smaller townhouse with the homeowner's association handling all the maintenance. Yippee—no more rototilling!

As long as I drove Rob's truck, I often felt that his strong arms were around me, protecting me. We had many wonderful years together, a deep understanding that often left words unnecessary, and things had to be tackled, good or bad, in an orderly, planned fashion. This way, rarely did we experience unpleasant surprises.

Helma's Story

On a different level, Lance and I often made decisions at a moment's notice without much ado or thought of the consequences. This process definitely allowed us to experience life to the fullest. I was so lucky to have experienced both of these men with their opposing points of view and ways to live.

As I mentioned, I am 75 years young now. During the past three years I have acquired two new hips, survived a heart attack and quit a two packs-a-day smoking habit of 54 years. I've lost the 30 pounds that I gained with the absence of cigarettes, and feel good. I still work two days a week in the same office I have worked in now for nearly 50 years to keep my mind exercised and open to all that is new. I marvel at all the new electronics and inventions. I still golf, which I took up (as well as bowling) in order to have hobbies that Rob and I could enjoy together.

Now golfing gives me a social life, fresh air, a venue to make new friends, and have a good time with my peers. I seem to be busy, even though I am semi-retired and, of course, people like Renette, make SURE I stay that way—just by asking me to try my hand at a small contribution to her new book.

During quiet times I love to remember the calm but strong time with Rob but also revel in the memories of the spontaneous and exhilarating times during my new widowhood with Lance in my life. I came out strong, learned that we women are—oh, so strong—and that a life with new adventures is mostly just around the corners. We just have to look!

Chapter 6

Marlene's Story

Four years ago, on November 28, 2007, my husband suddenly died. He had loved listening to a new song written by John Fogerty. The song begins with the words describing a foreseen phenomenon: "I dreamed I walked in heaven just the other night, there was so much beauty, so much light. Don't you wish it was true, don't you wish it was true?" Was it at coincidence, or did John really know?

I was born Marlene Rose Lefler in Flint, Michigan, on a warm October day. I was raised with my very close brother, Jimmy, in the small country town there of Mount Morris. My mom, Irene, is 100 percent Hungarian, born in America into a blue collar family. Her mother, Theresa Sari, passed away before I was born. Grandpa Sari lived with us until he became very old and fragile. He lived 94 years. Mom worked as a hotel maid in her younger years, then got a job in an auto factory on an assembly line. For a fun activity, she liked to go to dancing. In the 1940's many single couples who had a common interest like dancing met and fall in love, and so it was with my parents.

WW II was winding down and many servicemen were coming home. My dad, Lloyd, served in the military branch of the US Air Force. During the war, he was a staff sergeant/

mechanic and worked on P3 airplanes. Later he worked as a foreman in a spark plug factory. His heritage was a European mixture of Polish, Irish, and German. I was named after a famous song that he loved to hear during the war, *Lily Marlene*.

From kindergarten to sixth grade, I attended one-room country schools. Junior High was 7th and 8th grades and high school was 9th to 12th. My activities included basketball, softball, track, after school committees, Brownies, Girl Scouts, singing in a church choir, and cheerleading, for which I adopted the nickname, *Marty*.

At age 16, I worked my first job as a car hop, but with no roller skates. Michigan winters are sometimes bitterly cold, and that job involved serving food to people from outside of their cars. The owner of Wally's drive-in only closed one day of the year, on Christmas Day. One freezing day, I couldn't feel my fingers while making change for a customer. My fingers were paper white, and I remember how much I cried because of the stinging. I escaped frostbite by running my hands under cool water. The next day I quit that job.

I met my boyfriend in my sophomore year. He was a junior and the quarterback for our football team. His name was Doug, and he owned a car. Doug and I liked to go fishing and to the drag races. We went steady for about three years until he was drafted into the army and was stationed in Viet Nam.

I graduated from high school with a 3.2 GPA in a college-prep program. I wanted to become a nurse, but my parents wouldn't fund my college costs. My dad gave me $750 as a graduation gift from a cashed-in insurance policy and an application for the radiology school at St. Joseph Hospital in Flint. It was a two-year program with classroom education and on-the-job training. Only seven students were accepted after screening 20 applicants, and I was fortunate to be one of those chosen.

I funded the tuition with my dad's gift. The cost was $500 on tuition, and books for the first year. The second year the school paid me a monetary stipend because the students worked half of the day. I was 19 and in my second year of school when I moved out of the house after a major altercation with my mother. Somehow I could afford rent, a car payment, and shared living expenses with a roommate—all on $200 per month. Well, that was 42 years ago when the price of gas and bread was around 50 cents. My roommate was also a second-year student and her name was Brenda. We lived in a one-floor, two-bedroom apartment flat next to this huge empty house downtown.

It was a week before Christmas in December 1968, when a big snowstorm dropped several inches of white powder during the night. In the morning Brenda and I were pleasantly surprised as we walked out the door for school. There were two guys shoveling out our snow-filled driveway. "Who are you guys?" I asked. One replied, "I'm Jim, this is Tom, and we're from the Pi Kappa Alpha fraternity next door." Brenda and I looked at each other with big grins as I softly remarked, "We hit the jackpot!" They were attending General Motors Engineering Institute for three years and it was winter break when everyone went home for the holidays, which was why the house seemed empty. About 40 young men from all over the United States lived in this multi-room Victorian house, in a rotation of 20 students every six months. The rest of the year they returned to their hometowns to work. Brenda and I became acquainted with most all of them, primarily through parties and group functions, because of our status as the neighborhood babes. One evening, there was a knock at our door, and when I opened it there was a guy with a big smile on his face and a huge piece of chocolate cake in his hand. He introduced himself as Scot, and offered us girls a piece of his birthday cake. Scot was actually the last fraternity brother we met. He and I connected chemically, and dated for two years. I finished radiology school and he graduated from General Motors Institute as a Mechanical Engineer. We married in January 1971. Our life became disorganized because of Scot's job disinterest, and we relocated frequently from different states, including Maryland, Michigan and California—both Southern and Northern. After fourteen years of frustration and being physically abused, I divorced Scot. I have two children from the marriage. Vincent was 11 years old and Marlena was nine when we separated. Scot and I made a settlement on court-ordered terms, and I took the kids.

I have the belief that my soul has spiritual guides because in this lifetime whenever a door of opportunity shuts, another one opens. Something, someone, some form of energy helps me to find answers to my needs.

Living alone in Castro Valley, California, away from family with two small children, no job, and a home in foreclosure, I was desperate and depressed. I somehow found the energy to look for a job. I had the licensed skills and experience in radiology but I hadn't worked for several years because of chronically moving from state to state. The job market in my field was slim, and that coupled with my hiatus from employment, made job searching a difficult task. I sent resumes to every hospital and clinic within 50 miles. There was no response, but then one day I happened to pick up a local newspaper. There was job advertisement for a Special Procedure Radiology Technologist at a hospital in South San Jose. My eyes filled with tears and I felt a feeling of enthusiasm and hope. I just knew that this was it, and that my door of opportunity was opened. On December 18, 1985, one week before Christmas, I was hired and trained to work in the Cardiology Department to perform technical radiologic nursing procedures, and I have now been with the company for 26 years.

For the next five years I rented a three-bedroom house near the hospital where I worked. My children reestablished their lives as they changed schools and made new friends. Living as a single working mom, however, was quite a challenge. There were good times and frantic times. My kids were becoming teenagers and all mothers know how difficult it is to deal with problems at their age. I decided that I couldn't handle the stress of working and raising both teens alone. My son desperately needed his father's discipline so I asked Scot to take Vincent, who was then 16. They lived together in a house in Fremont. It was a good decision.

A year went by, and I developed a yearning to go to San Jose State University (SJSU) to complete my bachelor's degree. I had sporadically attended classes for years at several different schools due to the constant relocation during my marriage. From age 22 to age 42, I had acquired enough credits to enter college as a junior, and so I did. Now think about this. I worked full-time days, attended college in the evening and weekends, then managed my life as well as my daughter's life, and all the while doing homework. I lived like this for five years, and finally graduated with a 3.4 GPA. How did I do it? I haven't a clue. Why did I do it? Actually I think that I did it for two reasons. I needed to overload my life to avoid depression, and also I was driven by an energetic feeling of need to finish my education.

A Cinderella story
In the meantime, my job became profitable and stable. I worked a lot of overtime and received yearly raises and sometimes bonuses. I managed to save enough money to make a down payment on a condominium. Just imagine a single mother

struggling to survive in this world after losing everything in a divorce, then finding the opportunity to make enough money to own a piece of the American Dream.

I remember signing the closing papers in June 1995. My realtor gave me the keys to my new life. When I opened my door for the first time, I felt indescribable elation. I walked into a dream. There were spectrums of bright light shining through the windows and outside my balcony there was a beautiful landscape with fluffy green grass, fragrant flowers, and shady trees. It was a twelve hundred square-foot flat on the second level, built over my carport. It had two bedrooms, two baths, a full kitchen, an indoor clothes washer and dryer and brand new carpeting throughout. It was so well kept and new and I was only the second owner. As I walked into the living room where there was a fireplace, I found that the former owners left a Duraflame log in the grate as a housewarming gift. It was there in the middle of the room that I realized that I wasn't dreaming. Everything was real. I bought my first property and I did it all by myself.

Life is good and getting better and better
My daughter, Marlena, was about 15 going on 20. She made friends very easily around our new place, while I kept busy working and going to college. Nine years had passed since my divorce and I had dated only two men. Marlena frequently tried to introduce me to some of the men she met around the complex. I had no time for that. One late evening she didn't come home on time from a school function. There were no cell phones for communication at that time, so I had to go outside and look for her. It was getting dark fast and I was panicking. I finally heard her voice and found her at the pool side talking with a guy she wanted me to meet. It was her way to force our meeting because she knew that I would go looking for her.

His name was John Bolla, and he was lying on a reclining lounge chair drinking a beer. I guessed that he was in his early 40's. He was a slender attractive Portuguese man around 5'9" with thick, wavy, dark brown hair. He offered me the last beer from his cooler, and invited me to relax on a nearby lounge chair. After knowing that my daughter was safe, I accepted his offer and all three of us chatted and laughed about Marlena's sneaky trick. I learned that he was a meat cutter and that he managed the meat department at Lucky's supermarket. He rented the condo across the street from where I lived and he collected treasures from the dumpster, like discarded furniture. I also learned that he had a seven-year-old daughter from a relationship with a co-worker, and that he shared her custody. The thought of a middle-aged man with a hobby of dumpster diving raising a first-grader is not on my list of the most appealing men. But, John and I shared our life stories. He was the middle child of three children and was raised in a Portuguese town near Oakland. He had two previous marriages. The first marriage with his childhood sweetheart was successful for many years. They had four children together and owned two houses. He left and divorced because of financial reasons. He developed an estranged relationship with his family because the children never forgave him for leaving. His second marriage ended bitterly and left him with a huge debt because his wife charged the maximum on his credit cards before she left him. It took him five years to pay off the debt and left him almost homeless. At one point he said that he lived out of his truck and shared bathroom facilities with some friends. Although I wasn't as desperate as John was, I realized that we had similar experiences surviving a broken marriage.

Anyway, I kept busy working and going to school, and life was good

For the next six months, I encountered John from time to time, most frequently at the pool or in my travels while jogging.

I asked him to fix some equipment in my condo since he also worked part-time for the complex in maintenance. One Thursday afternoon, I was heading toward my car to go to the store and I found John spray painting a scratch on my front fender. I was so impressed with that nice gesture that I invited him to go with me to an indoor football game on Friday night. He hesitated to answer at first, but then he accepted my offer. It was our first date together and the beginning of our relationship. John had a very charismatic personality and I was easily seduced by it. He was jovial and magnetic. He had so much energy, and was constantly active. I describe him as having had the metabolism of a hummingbird. He was always moving the furniture around his home for a change. He started projects, and didn't finish them. When he was a kid in school he couldn't sit still in a chair for long so it was difficult for him to focus on his learning. These actions illustrate a condition called Attention Deficit Hyperactive Disorder. ADHD is a medical condition that makes someone more active than normal and makes it difficult for a person to concentrate. It also causes behavioral problems. He confessed that he had high blood pressure and was on medication for it. In spite of knowing John's shaky history our chemical bond grew strong, along with our feelings of compatibility. I think that my nursing background and ability to feel compassion for people overcame my reluctance to respond emotionally.

We discovered common interests together and shared romantic adventures like going to dinner and dance clubs because we clicked as dance partners. In the winter, we enjoyed going to go to the snow together. I would ski down the slopes, while he would snowboard. We had an unforgettable ski vacation/cardiology conference in Vail, Colorado, in January 1996. We passed sappy love notes by leaving them on the windshield of our cars and finding one (especially in the morning) was so exciting. I felt like a kid opening a Christmas present! I still have those notes in my treasure chest.

Marlene's Story

I love to play golf and, of course, John wanted to play as well. He didn't own golf clubs so I lent him an extra set that I had in storage. I reactivated John's interest in the game since he used to play golf when he was younger. He said that he played Pebble Beach when the cost was only $20.00. Now the fee is $340.00 and the player has to spend the night at the Pebble Beach Inn. We began to play golf frequently, so I bought John a one-year Duke's membership for his 45th birthday that allowed him to play three nice Monterey courses: Delmonte, Spanish Bay, and Spyglass. He loved that gift so much that this challenging pastime became a passion for him.

A year had passed since I met John, and we were in love. One day while playing golf, he mentioned that his landlord was going to raise his rent. John was very affected financially because of the debt he incurred from his second wife, so he asked to move in with me. I thought about it, and then I agreed because he would pay half of my mortgage and I would save money. I would also find out if I could live with him. Everything was beautiful and it seemed to be a good plan.

In December 1996, I finally graduated from college with a bachelor's degree in Health Care Management. I wanted to celebrate my long-awaited achievement, so I planned a wonderful trip for us. The following month, we sailed over the crystal blue Pacific waters on a Norwegian cruise ship to the Mexican Rivera. It was such a romantic vacation—so romantic that John asked me to marry him. I was very hesitant to answer. I had to think about being married again. It had been twelve years since my divorce, and I was 47 years of age. I had a secure job and I owned my own home, but yet I loved John and I wanted to grow old with a mate. I felt that marrying was the right choice for us, so we married on July 7, 1997 (7-7-97), at Harrah's Casino in Lake Tahoe. The number "7" has always been a lucky number for me. It also was the same month and day that my parents and my brother were married.

At the time, the housing market was priced at a low prime rate. I wanted to upgrade our lifestyle and buy a house. It was a time when a lot of people had the same thought, so we had to compete in price with everyone else in a bidding war. After searching for months to find the right house, I encountered a sweet deal. A friend from work told me that her neighbor was selling her home in Gilroy. She was putting it on the market the very next day. John and I visited the house that night, and agreed to the asking price. I sold my condo, and used the equity to make the down payment on the house. We closed the deal in Easter week of 1998 and moved from San Jose to the southern part of Santa Clara County. That move was the beginning of the end of our adventure together. John had become an equity investor and a home owner again.

If there is one constant factor in the universe, that factor is change

Several major changes occurred in these past five years of my life. I bought a condominium, met John, lived with him, graduated from college, got married, and then bought a house in Gilroy. These were wonderful changes, however, along with the good there is the bad. It is the counterbalance in the laws of physics. John was changing for reasons that I didn't understand at the time. He became argumentative, and he chose to sleep on the couch at night. He had a lot of excuses, and the best one was that he had insomnia because of his hyperactivity. I made dinner and he didn't come home to eat. He said that he already ate. He started to smoke cigarettes. I was in shock and disbelief at his actions. John knew how I despised that habit. I would have never married him if he smoked. He was drinking heavily. There is a bar and grill in Gilroy that my husband used to haunt known as Stinger's Saloon. John would hang out there almost every day. He acted like an alcoholic who only loves his alcohol. He was separating us by going to the bar every day and staying there into the night. There were times when I went to bed and woke

Marlene's Story

up around 10:00 p.m. or later and he still wasn't home. I would get out of my bed and drive my car to the bar to find him drinking Jack and Coke or throwing darts. There were women involved in these scenes, and I knew some of them. A few times he stayed out all night. His excuse was that he was too drunk to drive, so he slept in his truck. I questioned his conduct, but I could not drag him home. He denied having affairs with any women, but I later learned that all of his buddies knew he was cheating and they covered for him.

His behavior lasted for two years, and I was ready to leave him. It couldn't be a divorce because I would lose everything that I worked for all my life. John had melted into my life with no assets. I made more money than he, so I might have to pay him alimony. I had a nice savings and retirement account despite my having paid $35,000 for the down payment on the house. I would not give him half of my life savings, and I began to wonder if he planned this move from the beginning. I wondered if he was looking all along for a woman with money and a house to marry.

John became known as Johnny B. His signature song became "Johnny Be Good" which he played incessantly on the juke box in the bar. He bought a yellow Dodge truck known as the Rumble Bee along with a personalized license plate reading Johnny Bee. It was his icon that he associated with the Stinger's Saloon. He became a "leader of the pack," and he created a fellowship with the other barflies. His friends were known as "the circle of trust" because there were secrets among them, mainly John's secrets. This behavior finally escalated into our disconnection. I never knew this dark side of John, and I just couldn't stop it, no matter what I said. I felt that I was living in a nightmare. When I talked to those whom I thought were my friends about my situation, they just listened with little comment because they already knew about it. John had a charismatic personality, and they seemed to support him and his actions.

Learn from your mistakes

March of 2005 was the month and year. The time was 3:00 p.m. I was at work in the cardiac catheterization lab at Santa Teresa Hospital when I received a call from the emergency room that my husband was there with chest pain. When I met him there, he was sitting in a wheelchair and clutching his chest with his left arm. He was having a heart attack. The cardiac team performed an angioplasty that diagnosed him with major coronary blockages. Two drug-eluting stents were implanted for his re-vascularization. He was put on a blood thinner, a cholesterol controlling drug, and stronger blood pressure medication. He was discharged the next day, after the doctor lectured John severely. "You have to watch your diet, and you must quit smoking or you're going to die." He was a 55-year-old, going back to 21. He was living the life of Riley, and he wasn't going to change. He thought that the prescription drugs would protect him. No one from the bar knew about his medical condition, and I never mentioned it.

John continued to smoke Marlboro cigarettes and cigars, eat a high fat diet like greasy barbeque ribs with French fries, and drink booze heavily. He was also drinking Monster energy drinks which were another heart attack waiting to happen. He mentioned that one day he drank six cans of it. He had a level of energy as high as a five-year-old kid. I wondered if he was on drugs and I was very puzzled at this worsening behavior.

We pretty much lived separate lives by now. At one point I asked him the question, "Why are we still married?" He replied, "to pay half of the bills." After that remark, I assumed that I was only being used for him to live a comfortable life, while my life was miserable.

Marlene's Story

Two more years passed, and I had tolerated enough unhappiness with John and his friends. I went to the courthouse to collect legal separation papers. I would serve them to John and leave him with all the debts, or at least that was my plan.

The night before I was going to serve him the separation papers was a Wednesday night and five days after Thanksgiving. I had just returned home around 7:45 p.m. from a casual meeting with my friends from San Jose. I noticed that his Rumble Bee truck was parked in the driveway. As I closed the garage door, I realized that a light was on, so I reached to the wall to switch it off. Oh, my God! I saw the back of John's legs from a distance. I panicked, and ran to find him slumped over the garage sink. His arms were outstretched like Jesus as seen from the reverse side of a crucifix, and his head was turned and laying on his left arm. I instantly knew that he was dead because his jaw was dropped, mouth open, and his face was blue. There was no breath and no pulse. I frantically called 911 and the dispatch nurse told me to lay him on the floor and perform CPR. I collected my energy, and with tears streaming on my cheeks, I did it. He was only 57 years of age.

I need to explain, though, that even though John and I had dissolved our marriage, I still loved him. I never imagined that we would separate this way.

I was in shock and blubbering in disbelief now that he was gone. So many people were there at my house, and time passed so slowly. Phone calls were made to send the news to the circle of his friends. Everyone said the same thing. "I just saw him." He started drinking his booze at the saloon around noon that day, came home, and then died. This is not a pretty picture, but it is what happened. The pronounced cause of death written on his death certificate was a heart attack and hypertension. He was taking a high level of prescription medication, and he abused his health by using drugs, alcohol, and smoking.

There are people that come to you while you are grieving about a loss in your life. I believe that these messengers are meant to offer comfort, information, and advice, so listen and learn.

Four people came to me after John's death. Three were inside the circle of trust and one was outside the circle. Rick was John's close friend in the grocery business. I wanted closure over John's behavior, and an explanation of his lifestyle. Each of them confessed that John was cheating on me with other women. He was cheating for years. How does one deal with the dirty truth about all of the distrust and deceit? Unforgiving passion comes to mind. I especially will never forgive John's best friend for collecting his cell phone and offering to call his friends with the news so I wouldn't have to worry about it in my time of grief. The real intention, however, was to erase John's pictures and text messages from his girlfriends, particularly from Beth, who was married and worked at Stinger's as a bartender. The Gilroy gossips still talk about her bizarre behavior. She was so obsessed with John that she later bought a yellow Rumble Bee truck because it reminded her of John after his death. She created a shadow box and displayed all of John's favorite mementos at Stinger's. In it, there was a CD of "Johnny Be Good," a golf ball with tees, and other things that she adored about him, like his favorite gum and, of course, his picture.

John was just a simple man, but he made a lot of friends in Gilroy. He was gifted with a convincing personality and had magnetic energy. He must have enriched his circle of friends by giving them a reason to get together and play golf. Since his passing, Stinger's organizes an annual John Bolla Golf

Tournament which raises money for Veterans. John was never a member of a military branch and he died of a heart attack. It somehow doesn't make sense. Usually a personalized charity event raises money for research or a cure of an illness such as what killed John, heart disease.

Death happens in counts of three
Statistics have shown that it takes three years for someone to go through the grieving process after the death of a spouse. The most difficult loss is a husband or wife.

I was only in my fifth month of grieving for my husband when I received a call from my brother. My dear father passed away on April 29, 2008. I felt overwhelmed with the intense pain and loneliness in my soul. It is said that the death of a parent is the second-most difficult grief to process, and I was very close to my father. I remember loving him as my dad, my best friend, and my hero. He served in the Second World War, so he received a 21-gun salute at his funeral. I have an American flag encased in a shadow box in his remembrance. He lived to enjoy 89 years of life.

It just so happened that at this time that my son Vincent lost his job in the downturn of the economy. He also lost his house, and was in need of a place to stay in order to regain his status. So, Vince and his wife moved in with me, and they provided a huge comfort as well as company for me, and we supported one another for three years.

After learning about John's history of cheating, grieving about his death, and losing my dad, I cried all the time. I was so depressed that I only looked forward to sitting in my recliner chair with a glass of wine, just staring at the second hand on my clock ticking forward. My thoughts were mainly of the good memories of John before he changed, along with wonderful childhood memories with my dad. The more

I stared the more my mind wandered. The clock represented the time in our lives, and both time and life will go on with or without us. My emotions were clearly losing control. One morning I was lying in my bed in that foggy dream state when you are almost ready to awake, but not willing to awake. I clearly heard footsteps walk down the hall to my bedroom. The door opened, and I felt a presence. I was lying on my side with my back to the door. I felt someone sit on my bed, lie down beside me, and embrace me with a constricting hug. I was afraid because it felt so real, and I awoke expecting to see John. There was no one there. It was then I decided that I needed guidance to help me understand myself, so I found myself a therapist. April was an older lady around 70, and I bonded with her instantly. I spent at least a year with her counsel. April was my only real rescue from extreme depression because eleven months later in May of 2009, my 61-year-old brother suddenly passed away, just like John had. Jimmy had survived the Viet Nam War, and was awarded the Congressional Medal of Honor for extreme heroism. Except for my 92-year-old mother, he was my last real link to my family. I was crying impulsively without control, and I felt so empty and alone.

April explained to me that spontaneous crying was normal in the grieving process, especially after losing my husband, my father, and my brother within a year and half. She talked to me and comforted me while offering me Kleenex to wipe away my tears. She explained to me that all things must pass, and that I would heal with an understanding of the bigger picture. I learned that the universe offers a therapeutic energy and that I could reach into it from meditation. April offered me seven keys of advice to find happiness: 1) Build strong family relationships, 2) Maintain a secure and adequate financial situation, 3) Find rewarding and meaningful work or hobbies, 4) Cultivate new friends, 5) Focus on health, 6) Find the "zone"—that activity where you are completely engaged and absorbed in the moment, and 7) Be grateful for what you have. Life can be difficult and unfair; however, if you focus on these seven keys, you can improve your chances of living a good life and experiencing happiness.

I am a petite woman around 4'10" and 110 pounds with highlighted blond hair. I am 62 and still working in a major cardiac hospital in San Jose. I am immersed in work and fun hobbies, and living a fulfilled life. I travel on bicycle trips in other countries, and enjoy cultural events with my very close girlfriends, whom I consider my sisters. I go to breakfast and to dinner with my longtime friends, exercise, dance, go wine tasting, play golf, keep in contact with my children and grandchild, and volunteer to work at fun activities in Gilroy.

I have my health, my job, my house, my family, and my dear friends and I will be forever grateful for them. Kudos to all of us widows. We are not alone in this world or in the spiritual world. Thank you, Renette, for allowing me to express my happiness and sorrows during one of the most difficult times in my life.

Chapter 7

Stefi's Story

My name is Stefi Rudolph. I was born in Berlin, Germany on August 11, 1928. All of my family, including myself, is of the Jewish religion.

Adolf Hitler was in power in Germany from 1933 until his death, when he committed suicide in 1945. He made it very difficult for us to live in Germany as he hated the Jews and wanted to do away with them. He was responsible for killing six million in concentration camps. One day we received a phone call from my uncle, who lived across the street from us. and he told us that the Gestapo was on our block. My father was in the German army during the first World War, had served in the infantry fighting against the French, had been shot in his lung (that later in life entered his liver), and had been discharged with the "Iron Cross," the highest military honor medal. As the Gestapo came and pounded on our front door, my mother opened it and begged them on her knees not to take my father. They entered our home and went to see my father as he lay in bed. They were shown his x-rays in the drawer, and thank God they let him be.

Jewish children were not able to attend public schools in 1937, so I attended a Jewish school then. We wanted to leave the dictatorship to immigrate to the USA, but under the rules of President Roosevelt, we needed a sponsor for our family of four persons. My parents stayed up most of the nights then writing to people that might be able to help us. My father had a cousin in Long Island, NY, so he wrote to her, requesting her to sponsor us, but she did not have enough money, so she asked a friend if she would sponsor us.

This was not enough for four persons, and my parents' desire was to go to San Francisco, so they went to the American Embassy where they requested to leave Germany. It so happened that the immigration agent recognized my father's name and said, "Aren't you the man that had dancing lessons with my sister? Since my sister lives in San Francisco, I will write to her and see if she will sponsor you and your family to come to San Francisco. This chance meeting with him was a blessing for us, and his sister did sponsor us. My parents, my sister (who was 17 years old at the time), and I managed to leave Germany for America in June of 1939. On our ship were young German children that were being sent ahead as their parents wanted their children's safety. The parents had stayed behind and many most likely never saw their children again. There was a counselor aboard who would play with this group of kids. As kids like to be with kids, I went to watch them at the door. When they finished playing and it was time to go to bed, they started to leave, but I was still standing at the door, so the counselor said to me, "Didn't you hear what I said?" I answered him, "I am here with my parents," and that made me very proud. Remember, I was still so young at the age of ten. When we landed in New York Harbor, I remember my father kissed the ground with happiness that we all had made it to the "Land of the Free" and the "Land of Opportunities." My dad had friends that lived in Bethlehem, PA, that he had contacted to meet us at the pier in New York. This was so that my sister and I could stay with them while we waited for the ship connection to

SF, as that was not until early September. So, we went with complete strangers to their home in Pennsylvania.

As we were leaving, we were asked to go and sit in the back seat of their car. I put my head on my sister's lap and cried. This couple was ever so sweet and caring toward us for the next two months until they drove us back to New York City where my parents had rented a very small apartment with the small amount of money we had. We only had $16.00 total upon entry in the U.S.A. because Hitler's government had taken all of our other finances away including jewelry, my Star of David amongst it. That is why we had made all financial arrangements with the ship lines while we were still in Berlin, and were able to book ourselves into First Class.

We arrived in San Francisco in late September. My sister, Ilse, and I stayed with the couple that helped us to get to America, and we were there until my parents moved into a flat that had been pre-arranged by these nice sponsors. We also had to wait until our belongings that were shipped from Germany via Costa Rica arrived. That took quite a long time. When they arrived, the dishes were mostly broken. We had already heard them break when they were being packed as the workers stepped on the boxes. They did not care—all they wanted was just to make more room. After the crates arrived and were unpacked, Ilse and I finally joined our parents. The rent for the flat was being paid by our sponsors and my dad said, "After I have an income, I will pay everything back," which he did once they had a steady income.

Our dad worked very hard. Somehow he got hold of some men's neckties, and would go from house to house, business to business to sell those neckties. Awhile later, he got a job in a warehouse for the Schilling Spice Company where he worked packing vanilla bottles. He developed a rash from the contents of some broken bottles. Later, he worked for McKesson and

Robbins, a pharmaceutical company. From there he was able to retire, but the work had been hard on him as he was in a cold warehouse always nearly freezing.

Mother worked in the beginning doing dishes for people after parties. She asked me to help her dry them, but told me, "Please be careful and don't drop and break any, as we will have to pay for them." After that job, she was able to find work in an insurance company. (I don't think I ever told you that she had never worked in her lifetime as Dad had made a good living in Germany for his family.)

My parents wanted for Ilse to have a profession, so they managed to send her to a beauty school to learn how to style hair. She graduated from there and found a job almost immediately in a beauty shop. In the meantime, I went to grammar school. I had lost almost two years of time in grade school as a result of the Hitler regime. I graduated from George Washington High School in 1947, after making up a grade in summer school.

During vacation time, I helped out in different jobs, working in a five-and-dime store, for AT&T as a telephone operator, and then went full time for a bank as a bookkeeper. My girlfriends and I went out to movies and roller skating at the beach for entertainment then. This was right after the war, and we met nice sailors there and dated a few just like all the other girls did and just had fun.

In October of 1948, I attended a dance at the Jewish Community Center in San Francisco, which was usually a special dance after Yom Kippur. Yom Kippur is the most important Jewish holiday of the year when you ask God to forgive the sins one has committed. That evening was always attended to full capacity. As usual, the ladies all stood on one side of the dance hall and the men on the other. I had already been asked to dance several times when this very handsome man came to me and asked me to dance. Of course, I did not refuse. He danced with me the rest of the evening and when he asked me if he could take me home, I said, "Yes." I only lived about four or five blocks from the center, so we walked as he did not have a car, although streetcars were available. I had many more dates with him following that evening.

One night after that, he came over to our house and brought me a box of candy. As I opened it, I saw a fancy piece wrapped separately in the center. When I went for that piece, it was hard to get out because he had fastened it to the box. By the way, my parents were in on all this. When I finally removed the piece of candy, there was an engagement ring in it, and needless to say, I was so surprised. Of course, I was very happy, and gave him a big hug and kiss. This friend, Al, now my fiancé, made such a wonderful impression on all of my family that it was unbelievable. We were both so young then—he was 21, and I was 20.

My job at that time was in a bank, and he was working for his brother-in-law in the family furniture store where he had been since he was 15, learning to upholster furniture.

I never believed in long engagements, so we got married in February 1949 and had a beautiful wedding ceremony at the Temple, with a reception at the Fairmont Hotel. We went to Yosemite on our honeymoon, but we did not have very warm clothes and had to return to our cabin often to warm up (you can imagine the teasing that we received from the other guests there).

When we returned from Yosemite, our lives began to change. I went back to the bank to work, and Al went back to the furniture store, but a little later, in 1952, he decided to leave his employment there and go on his own installing draperies, a craft he had learned. We were blessed to have three wonderful children—Sharon, Gary and Denise. After living in different apartments, some in S.F., we decided to put a down payment on a house in Daly City. As we watched it being built, it made us very happy to see what we had achieved.

In the beginning, Al constructed a work bench in the basement where he would cut drapery rods to size and sell with small orders. As our business grew, we bought even more fabrics to sell to our customers. He had an offer to set up a drapery department at another store in Daly City that was very successful, but the owner of that store later decided to have his own drapery department.

Al's dream was to have his OWN store, though, so we looked around and found a good location to set up the business on Mission Street in Daly City, where he was already known in the area. That was in 1964. We hired an installer at the start so that Al would be free to do the selling. I was working in the office, taking care of the books. I was quite efficient at bookkeeping, like I am in a lot of things that I do.

We created a nice showroom with a workroom in the back of the store where the seamstress would do the work. We hired one or two more salespeople, and made a very comfortable living. Our two eldest children came to work for us after their college education, but without any pressure from us. We had a successful business at that location for many years.

At the beginning of 1989, Al was not feeling well, so we went to the doctor and he was diagnosed with Pancreatic Cancer. This was a shock to all of the family. This stopped him from working so hard, staying home at times, but the kids and I kept the business going. In June of that year, we had made reservations to go to Maui. The doctor did not think that was a good idea, but we went anyway. Al told me, "I want to go there for you," so we did go, but it was very hard for him. While we were sitting on the balcony of the condo, he kept closing his eyes, listening to the waves, and that was very relaxing for him. We stayed there for about a week, and when we returned home he stayed mostly in bed. I wanted to be by his side, but he always told me to go to the shop and help the kids. I would phone him periodically, though, just to hear that he was OK.

My dear Al passed away during the early part of July in 1989 at home, with his family by his side. The Rabbi was phoned, and he came over immediately. He gave all of us a lot of support and was very compassionate, especially during the first few months, and so were some of my good friends. My kids and I kept the business going, but after awhile there was a discussion, and Sharon thought it would be best for her to go on her way independently. So, Gary and I worked together until I retired in 1998. Business was not too good after that, and the rent was high, so Gary looked around for another place to move to. Living in San Carlos and commuting to Daly City was always a chore with the traffic. He was able to find a space in San Mateo, though, where he is established at the present time, and his wife works with him, so it really stayed "a family business."

I am very proud of the outcome, and I know Al would be so pleased to know that the business he built up is still going after 59 years.

Don't let anyone tell you that it is easy to become a widow, but if you have children that are your best supporters, and that keep you young or sisters and/or brothers that are there for you when you need them, then that is half the battle, and you can go on with your life and try to stay healthy and happy.

Chapter 8

Becky's Story

Becky's Mom and Dad

My mother was born on the Island of Manhattan in New York City. Her parents were Victor and Julia Carmona. She was a petite woman, only five feet two inches with brown hair and brown eyes. She had a great personality, and everybody who met her loved her.

My mom's passion was singing, and she sang all the time while doing dishes, the laundry, and even when she was cooking. She never graduated from high school, but at the end of the eighth grade, she went to work in the garment district sewing nightgowns. Her own mom worked for a fashion house sewing sequins and jewels on lavish fabrics. My mom even tried out for a Broadway musical when she was eighteen.

My parents had seven children, with me being the oldest. She had three girls first, and then four boys. My dad wanted a boy and got his wish four times over! My mom truly was the best—working all the time and never complaining. She always said that she was worth seven million dollars because of her children. She was great.

My dad was born on the Island of Rhodes, which was then under Turkish rule. He was a very handsome man with a great head of black hair, and he wore it straight back like George Raft (remember him)? He came to the United States in his early twenties, or so he said. In those days they lied about their age, because they had to be old enough to work.

My father settled in Los Angeles, California, because his brother was already there. He went into the flower business selling flowers on the streets. They still do that today! One of my father's strengths was that he spoke six languages: Greek, Spanish, Italian, Turkish, English, and Hebrew. This helped him through his entire life. One of his passions was playing cards. Whether at home or in a card house, he could always manage to get a game together.

On Sunday evenings we would all get together with friends for potluck dinners and the men would play cards. This was a weekly ritual with no babysitters. The kids all came, too, and it was fun for everyone. Another thing about my dad was that when he would play cards in the afternoon, and if was a winner, he would always stop by the bakery and buy us a cake.

My dad was a strict man but a complete family man. On my dad's thirty-sixth birthday, I was thirteen years old, and decided to make him a cake, and what was so funny was that I used up the whole box of candles. In those days, there were 36 candles to a box and I could not believe I used the whole box. Today I always smile when I put candles on a cake, because it reminds me of my dad's 36th birthday.

I got my Mother's personality, for which I am quite thankful. My father's old fashioned values instilled a great work ethic in me.

Becky's Story

All about Becky

I was born in Los Angeles, California, on September 8, 1929. I was the oldest of the seven children. When I was five years old, we moved to Oakland where my father opened a floral shop at the corner of Thirty-Fifth Avenue and Foothill Blvd. We lived in the back of the shop, and had to climb out of the living room window to get to the shop! That was fun.

I attended Jefferson Grammar School and Alexander Hamilton Junior High, both in Oakland. We moved to San Francisco when I was in the eighth grade. Because of the war, flowers were scarce and so my folks opened a "mom and pop" produce store at 20th and Geary in the city. There I attended George Washington High, and during my senior year I worked what they called the 4-4 plan: working four hours and going to school four hours a day.

Just before graduating, I went to work for Wells Fargo Bank. I loved my job, and learned about all the different departments. I worked in bookkeeping, bank books, the clearing house, and finished up being what they called a "float." That was the best job of all because they would send me to all different departments and it helped me learn all the bank officer's tasks so that I was able to take over when they went on vacation.

Just a little side note: I met a future celebrity while working at Wells Fargo. Her name was Barbara Huffman, who won the Miss San Francisco pageant. You would know her as Barbara Eden of *I Dream of Jeannie* fame. I've never contacted her but I recall her telling me, "I wish I had your legs!" That was funny to me, and I never forgot it.

One of my favorite things to do was go ice skating on Friday and Saturday nights at Sutro Baths at the beach. I met my first husband there. His name was Frank Berkovatz.

He was very handsome with red curly hair and a great smile. Gorgeous! We dated for about eight months and married in Carmel.

Before we were married, Frank had been in the army. He was stationed in Germany in the Bavarian town of Garmisch—Partenkirchen where he was an apprentice butcher. After he got out of the service, he was entitled to buy a house under the GI bill. The year was 1955, and we were living in an apartment in San Francisco, so one day we decided to look for a house to buy. We started driving down the peninsula, and the first city that had sunshine was San Bruno. We were lucky to find a new development near the city park that had model homes. The prices were in our range, so we started looking at the models. Frank and I found one we both liked and the next thing we knew we were picking out a parcel. We selected one that would be built in eight months. This gave us extra time to save more money to put this all together. Frank Jr., our first son, arrived on October 31st 1956 (on Halloween) and our second son, Jeffery was born September15, 1958.

I stayed home for six years raising our sons. Because money was tight, though, I wanted to go back to work. I didn't want to go back to the bank because it was too far to commute, but there was a brand new coffee shop opening up in downtown San Bruno called Lyon's. I applied for a job as a waitress but because I had no experience they told me no. They suggested I consider a hostess/cashier job and I said, "I can count money and have worked for a bank." They called that night and told me I had the job.

While I was working there, I met a man named Harold Highsmith who was a realtor. He had an office in San Bruno, thought I had a great personality, and asked me if I would consider working as a real estate salesperson. He even offered to sponsor me! My sister-in law was in real estate, and I

Becky's Story

thought, "If she could do it, I can too." I enrolled in a real estate school in San Mateo the very next week. By November of that year I took the exam in San Francisco and I passed the test. I gave a two week notice at the coffee shop, and started working in the real estate business on January 4, 1964. I sold my first house by the end of that month.

During these years, Frank worked at a brewery in Oakland for many years. He was also a very good house painter so our home was always in great condition. After 17 years, Frank and I went our separate ways. Real estate was my salvation! Meeting and helping people is very rewarding to me and what I love to do.

All about Ken
Ken was born on August 21, 1929, in Joplin, Missouri. Both of his parents were from Missouri, too. His father was a traveling salesman for Swift & Company, and his mom was a housewife. She was an excellent bridge player, but she was definitely not a good cook. Ken spent his school nights at home because his mom was afraid to stay alone in the evenings, and so Ken would read all kinds of books to keep himself busy. In high school he was on the debate team, and won many honors for his school.

Ken started playing golf with his dad at the young age of eight. He idolized his dad.

Ken entered the Navy as soon as he graduated from high school, and he married at age nineteen, had his first daughter at age twenty, and then he and his first wife had twin girls four years later.

He spent most of his working life as the owner of gas stations and a truck stop in the Bay Area. In 1973, Ken was in a propane explosion at one of his gas stations trying to help one of his customers start his trailer. There was a leak, and before he knew it, an explosion occurred and Ken was badly burned. Ken was hospitalized in intensive care for more than three months, severely burned on his face and hands. They tried a new treatment on him. The treatment was an acid solution, which left him with no scars whatsoever. The treatment was very painful, but the results were miraculous. Ken's first wife passed away, so Ken married again, and that marriage produced two more girls—five daughters in all. At the age of 50, Ken decided to retire because the government was demanding gas station owners conform to new regulations. His second marriage did not work out, so they divorced in 1983.

Ken and Becky
While working in real estate, my boss, Don Bennett, belonged to the Green Hills Country Club in Millbrae, CA. One day he came into the office with his golf buddy, Ken. He was retired and wanted to stay busy, so he started working in real estate. One day while I was holding an open house, Ken came in. I was surprised to learn that he lived right around the corner. It was July 3, 1983, and that's a date I always remember. The very next day, I was holding the same open house, and near closing time. Ken walked in, and told me that he picked up all my open house signs, and that it was time to close up and go with him to have a drink. It was July 4, after all! I accepted his invitation, and that is how our friendship started.

We married three years later on his father's birthday (Flag Day-July 14, 1986). We soon moved to Lake Wildwood, near Grass Valley, in the foothills east of Sacramento. Being up in the pine trees and by a lake was wonderful. We had a great home with cedar shingles and dark green trim. I called it our "Carmel House." Because our house was on a golf course, we added a pool in the front yard. I did all the landscaping, but was unaware the deer would be visiting us and eating

Becky's Story

all the flowers. We learned the hard way. We enjoyed our life there, and had many barbecues with friends and family. My grandchildren learned to swim in that pool, and learned to play golf with me on that course.

We traveled the world, and played golf everywhere we went. Ken would say some men would give their eye teeth to have played on the courses we had. We were very lucky! As we traveled, I collected golf hats and spoons.

In 1999, we moved to the desert, calling the Springs Country Club our home. Ken loved the course there. Hal and Ruth, our best friends, lived here, too. By joining the golf club, we met so many wonderful people, and today they are still active friends. My true friends were there for me when my husband passed away, and I am very thankful for all the support they gave me.

Our last two trips together were to South Africa to golf, and go on a safari. A grand trip! The very last trip was a cruise to Russia and Italy. We were lucky.

Coping with his illness
When Ken had his first stroke, we were on our way home from Maui, just before Thanksgiving in 2005. We had booked the last flight of the day from Maui to San Francisco. Up until that last leg of the trip, Ken was feeling fine. Ken felt something was wrong on that flight from SF to Palm Springs. It started with numbness in his right arm, and by the time we got to Palm Springs, he was paralyzed on his entire right side. The flight attendants carried him off the plane, and called paramedics. He was rushed to the hospital, and received medical attention right away. They ran countless tests, but found no sign of why he had the stroke, and he didn't suffer any side effects, such as a limp or slurred speech. We were very lucky.

We thought things were going to be okay, but two weeks later Ken had another stroke. He fell off the chair while watching TV, and could not get up. Luckily my son, Franco, was there to help him up. We called, the paramedics showed up, and they took him to Eisenhower Hospital. Again, there were more tests, but they could not detect the cause of the stroke. Very frustrating.

Ken got better, and returned to the golf course, but did not enjoy it as much because he could no longer play as well. This went on for five years or so. We would often watch golf and football on TV together, and it would always tickle me when Ken would call the penalties before the referees did, and the announcers would confirm Ken's calls. He would say when there was an interception, the quarterback was telegraphing the play by looking at the receiver. Ken's mind stayed sharp, and he was able to play dominoes at the club, and he really loved it when he won. Ken stayed competitive 'till the end.

In October 2010, Ken was diagnosed with tumors under his left jaw (stage 4). Ken refused the recommended treatments. He felt at age 81 that he had lived a great life. His first wife had died of cancer even after taking the treatments, and that may have influenced his decision.

The last two months of Ken's life we called in Hospice and it was the best thing we did. At first Ken objected as he felt we did not need them, but he signed the papers anyway. At first they came only one day a week to see how he was doing, but he still felt it was not necessary. They stopped coming because he was eating on his own, and not losing weight. Two weeks later, though, he took a turn for the worse and we had Hospice return on a regular basis. On his final day, I took our stereo into the bedroom so he could listen to his favorite station. When he heard the music, he smiled. Ken passed away on February 3, 2011.

Becky's Story

The celebration of life was held at our home on March 13, 2011. Ken's lucky number was 13, and that's how we picked that date. Ken's best friend, Hal, took charge of everything. All of our friends came and it helped a great deal.

God Bless you, Ken. See you in Heaven.

Staying busy
Believe me when I say losing your husband is difficult. Being alone is hard, and coming home to an empty house is tough, to say the least. We had been together 24/7. We did everything together.

For the first few months, I really did not do much. Playing Mah Jongg helped. I played twice a week with Gwen, Doris & Roberta. Keeping your mind busy is the key. I love playing games, so I would ask my friends over for lunch and we would play gin rummy or Mah Jongg. Going to the movies with friends also helped.

I am lucky to have a family that cares. At first they came to visit me and stayed for a while. They took turns, as they did not want me to be alone. I finally said, "I am going to be okay."

Today I am back in real estate. I sold real estate before I met Ken, and I kept my real estate license active all those years. I have always enjoyed selling real estate, meeting people, and helping them find their dream home. The real estate business has really changed since I was last in it. It's all about the computers now. All the listings and purchase agreements are done on a computer. The first thing I had to do was hire a computer tutor, and I was lucky enough to find a good one, Daniel. After returning to real estate, I was lucky to sell my first property to a great couple from Wisconsin while holding an open house in Mission Hills. The real estate market is turning around, and we are all happy for it. AMEN.

I still love to cook and bake, especially my butter cookies, which I give to others during the holidays. I also enjoy playing golf with my friends.

A lot of my friends have lost their husbands, so we try to help each other by phoning each other often, and making sure everyone is okay. If I did not have real estate, I probably would be working at Eisenhower Hospital as a volunteer or something like that, maybe working in the gift shop. There are a lot of things one can do to keep busy, you just have to look where you can be most helpful.

Footnotes to my story
Renette and I both graduated from George Washington High School, Class of 1947, in San Francisco. We both ice skated at Sutro Baths and were members of the speed skating club called the Silver Blades.

Danny, Renette's husband, had his first job working for my uncle at the House of Flowers in San Francisco. At our fiftieth high school reunion we connected again, and I asked her if she played golf. She said yes, so I invited her to my house in Lake Wildwood to play in a tournament. It got rained out, but we had a good time anyway.

Today I am five feet five, size fourteen, have no butt, but good legs, olive skin, and white blond hair. I have lost weight since my husband passed away, so I am getting wrinkles. So what! I've been told that I don't look my age. I do have a good personality, and a great attitude and smile. I'm having a wonderful life, and it 'aint over yet.

Chapter 9

Mona's Story

Once upon a time, a young, forty-two-year-old woman fell in love with her knight in shining armor.... Sounds like a good tale, doesn't it? But, I had better back up and give you a little background on myself before I begin to tell you about this remarkable love affair.

I was born in Topeka, Kansas. My parents were very young—seventeen and eighteen. My dad was in the service, and my mom was a waitress where all the cute young soldiers hung out on their time off. (Well, there is a love story all of its own!) My mom met my dad and fell in love, they got married, and then had me.

Mom loved to tap dance and entertain, and Dad was still in the Army, so after I was born I lived with my grandparents and my young aunts for the first four years of my life. Of course, Mom came and went as she needed to. One day, however, Mom got mad at Dad, and moved to California with me. She later remarried, though, and then I had a stepfather and a stepsister.

As I said, my mom loved to tap dance, so she opened up a studio and gave lessons. Not surprisingly, my sister and I learned to tap dance from the time we were very young. We danced in talent shows, school plays, and recitals at school. Life went on and, at a young age, I got married and had my three children. As life happens, I was married for nineteen years, and then divorced.

Bill A. Wolters was born in Chicago, Illinois. His mother was Lithuanian, and his father was German. Bill had a brother and sister a little younger than himself. When Bill got out of high school, he moved to California and worked for a telecommunications company. He was a very energetic young man, decided he wanted to be his own boss, and started a company called Wolters Communications while he was living in San Jose. He married and had two boys. He eventually divorced and moved to Watsonville, California, where we met.

I was a young, divorced woman with three children to raise on my own, all at the age of thirty-eight. I had gone to beauty college during my marriage, so now I decided I would get serious about my career. I got a loan, and opened up a beauty salon in Watsonville, and I called it Mona's Sheer Delight. Catchy, huh? I worked many hours at the shop, which didn't leave me much time to date. I did go to church and had many nice friends, and I dated once in a while, but never anyone special.

At the time, my two sons, Jeff and Brian, were teenagers, and my daughter, Kimberly, was nine. Jeff and Brian both had jobs, but my daughter went to school so I tried to be home when she got home. I had great in-laws that were a big help to me if I had to work late. Of course, in the beauty business there can always be some long hours required, and it wasn't always easy on my children, but we managed.

My best friend is named Sharon, and we had a lot of fun times together, sometimes along with her husband, Jim.

Sharon and Jim had a daughter, Christen, who was the same age as my Kimberly, so the two of us often did things with our girls, too.

The trip
Sharon and I went on a trip to Solvang one year and then traveled on to Hearst Castle. We had a nice weekend—a girl's weekend out. We saw a show one night starring Neil Diamond. It was a very romantic show. Well, he can melt any woman's heart and can he sing! Of course, he got the girl in the end and drove a "White Corvette" out into the sunset. I knew then my special guy would have to have a "White Corvette." I told Sharon my next boyfriend would have to have a car like that, and we laughed.

Back to work
I had several women working in my beauty salon and one of the gals, Patricia, invited me to go out to shoot some pool, have a glass of wine, and just have some fun. So I did. That night a friend of hers named Bill Wolters was there having a good time just shooting pool and hanging out with his friends. Well, I couldn't keep my eyes off of him. He was 6'2," had the longest legs, and was very good looking. He was a couple of years older than I was.

I tried not to be too conspicuous in admiring him, and found out later that he was quite smitten with me, too. It wasn't long after that pool night that Bill took his two sons to lunch at the pizza parlor next to my shop. Patricia mentioned to me Bill was there, so I made an excuse to go talk to the parlor owner whom I knew well. I tried to act nonchalant, but I just had to check him out again. After I left, he and his boys left shortly after, and guess what he was driving? Yes. You guessed it. A white Corvette! So, I knew that was my man. Patricia told me that the night we were playing pool Bill told her husband he was going to ask me out. So, a few days after the encounter at the pizza parlor, Bill called and asked me if I would go out with him. I was naturally very excited, but tried to sound very casual, and said I would like that. When I asked him when, he said, "Yesterday," and I thought that was cute. But, we decided on the following Saturday.

What to wear
Bill seemed very distinguished to me, so I knew I had to have the perfect outfit. I was the kind of young woman that liked to look sexy, but not too sexy, and not too cute. What a dilemma! I finally settled on a dress I felt good about, not too sexy, but not too cute. The big night came and we went to Club 21 in Soquel, CA. I was too excited and hardly ate my dinner. Bill had also invited his best friend, Richard, and Richard's girl friend. I think Bill was a little nervous, too, but the night went well. We danced and had a great time. After that night we were practically inseparable. What a guy he was!

We had many dates after that. When Bill went on one of his business trips, he called my shop the day after he had left and told my shop manager that he had purchased a ticket for me, and I should get on that flight to come up and meet him. It was another difficult decision as to what to wear on a trip like that. I finally managed to get it together, though, and met him in Seattle Washington. Then I attended one of his meetings with him, he was so professional and businesslike, but when we were alone he could be quite a character. You wouldn't know he was the same person. I learned a lot about the telecommunications business back then.

He traveled quite a bit with his small company, Wolters Communication, Inc. His company fluctuated in size, depending on the strength of the economy. At the time, he was doing some business with Pac Bell, some with Verizon (which was then GTE), as well as with other, smaller companies. Bill loved to golf and was just a fun loving kind of guy, so besides some business trips together, we did a lot of fun trips with his golfing. We would go to Tahoe often, for example. We were both fairly quiet people, so when we went to parties Bill would always say we should sit with people that would talk a lot.

We also did interesting things together such as taking music lessons at Cabrillo College. Bill was great in the theoretical part of music; he could easily grasp the fundamentals of music, and the structure, but when it came to singing or playing an instrument, he had no interest. I was the one that did the singing. I wasn't exactly Christina Aguilara material, but it was fun. We took dance lessons which we enjoyed, and also took a computer class together.

My boys were in their early 20s by then, busy working in construction, and busy with their own lives, while Kimberly was still at home with me. One of Bill's boys still lived with him. It isn't always easy to blend families together, but we wanted to try. We had been dating about a year when we decided to live together.

The Question
Well, it wasn't "The Question" you would think of off the top of your head. One night when we were out to dinner, Bill wanted to know how I felt about having a baby. Wow! Here I was at age forty three, and he was two years older. But, I decided I would like to have a child with him. Crazy, huh? We talked about it often, and even consulted with my doctor. At our ages, should we do this? Over many dinner discussions, we "officially" decided to try (not that we hadn't already tried). We didn't want to tell anyone yet, especially Bill's mom.

In the meantime, we each had our own work and our wonderful children to enjoy. I continued working at the beauty salon and Bill continued in the telecommunications business. He still traveled some and played a lot of golf, but he always had time for me and his ten-year-old son who lived with us. My daughter, Kimberly, was on her own by then, and the other children were grown and on their own, except Bill's daughter who still lived with her mother.

Down to business
The main branch of our business was at our home in Watsonville. I say our business because I started working in the business when Bill and I became close. Actually I hadn't become part of the business yet other than working with Bill in the office. Our home was kind of remote, we had a lot of property, and neighbors were fairly scarce around us. But it was nice. We played enough that when we were home we appreciated it. We always seemed to have plenty of company and kids coming and going.

The business was down to a one or two customers, such as GTE at that time, which became Verizon and AT&T. These customers have projects nation wide. Bill had a handful of people working in the different areas at the time around the nation. Bill had to work on the idea of either enlarging the company or doing something else. Well, you know how guys are. He wanted to make this business venture work since that is all he had done most of his life. He had a great business mind, though, and came up with the idea of hiring retired, experienced telephone men. Most of them had retired from telephone companies at an early age because they received a great retirement package, and after a few years of retirement they were ready to do something again. Our first retired employee was in Washington. Now, the idea was that it was a part-time job that gave our employees something to do, they had extra money coming in, and also kept our business alive. What a concept! After success in Washington we hired more men across the nation as area managers, and they would hire the people needed for projects in their area. That turned out to be a great idea, but, needless to say, it did become more than a part-time job for most of the managers.

Trying to build business further, we decided to become a woman-owned company. At this time I became 51% owner of the company. A woman owned company is a government effort (along with minority-owned companies) to help small companies succeed and generate business. In order to obtain that status, I had to get a contractor's license. Mine would be what they call a low-voltage license. I had to own 51% percent of the business for the company to qualify. I went back to school to learn about OSHA, all the office duties, and learn a lot about how everything worked in the field that we provided for the customers. I studied very hard to get my license, and even wore headphones to study when I worked out. I went to classes two or three times a week until I was ready to go to Sacramento to take the test. When it was finally time to go to Sacramento and take the test, I stayed at a nice hotel where many of the other test-takers stayed beforehand. I settled into my room, then went to work out since there was a gym within walking distance. When I came back from the gym, had a nice dinner, then went to my room to study a little more and get a good night's sleep.

I was pretty nervous, even though I had taken a state test before to get my hairdresser's license. This was quite different. The next morning I went to the building where they were giving the test. There must have been five hundred people there to take their contractor's test. Pretty scary. But, by the time I left the room I knew I had passed the test. It just felt right.

At that time, you didn't find out for several weeks if you passed or not. Now you know right away. If you don't pass the first part of the test, you cannot go on. You have to take it again another day. But, I went home feeling fairly confident and happy with myself.

We had won a big job in Hawaii and needed to hire an area manager and about forty workers, so we hired a gentleman named Mr. Higa since he was well known in Hawaii. He became a great asset to our team, successfully installing a telephone system at the University of Hawaii.

It was during our time in Hawaii that I found out I had passed the test and had my license. That was great news! We celebrated with our new manager in Hawaii.

When we returned home after the trip, there were balloons all over the house and office. Our office manager had decorated for the happy occasion. In the meantime, I still had a beauty salon to run. Fortunately, I had a very reliable assistant that took care of things for me in my absence.

About that time, we discovered that we were pregnant. So, now came the big question: "Marriage?" We decided it was time to get married, but we still hadn't told anyone except our minister about our plan to have a child together. I told my mother and Bill finally told his mother. They were both quite shocked. Our minister almost gave it away during the ceremony. But I am jumping ahead a little—I wanted to tell my daughter Kimberly first. She was my baby, and I didn't know how excited she would be about my being pregnant. So, I bought some flowers and a really cute, big-sister card, and took her out to lunch to share the news with her. Being the kind of person she is, she was quite elated about the news. Over the years she proved to be a wonderful big sister and enjoyed her baby sister a lot. I did tell my boys too, of course, but I knew they wouldn't be too upset over it.

Mona's Story

We had a wonderful wedding—way too large, probably, but how do you leave anyone out on such an important day? Our wedding took place at our home in Watsonville; we had a large two-story home in the Moss Landing area. Our business was located in a room off of the house.

We told everyone about our blessed event after the wedding, and I think most of our friends and family thought we were crazy. We went through all of the tests you have to take at that age, and waited for the results. We were both happy with the news when the doctor called and said everything was fine. Did we want to know the sex? Of course we did! She was exactly what we both wanted. We had boys and girls between us and we both wanted this little girl.

Life went on as we waited for this little girl. In the meantime, though, we had our work and our other wonderful children to enjoy. I continued working at the beauty salon, but I was also very involved in the company. I worked in the office along with an office assistant. I had to maintain hands-on control in the company in case someone came around to make sure there was a woman still running the business. Bill continued traveling to meet with his existing customers and traveling to the areas where we had Area Managers to build and meet with new customers. He also played a lot of golf. At that time taking the customer out for a round of golf was good for interacting with them.

My passion was working out, and Bill's was golf. He told me early on that I didn't have to golf with him, and I could just do my usual workout. He liked the fact that I stayed in shape and, of course, I liked his shape. Wherever we went, he would make sure I had time for a workout. One year we went to England, Scotland and Ireland. We traveled with three other friends of Bill's on that memorable trip and we saw many castles and, naturally, golf courses. The guys played golf while I shopped, worked out or just hung out in the lounge and read a book. I had to learn to drive on the left side of the road there, and that was a trip! It was beautiful country, and we often stayed at B&Bs with an occasional hotel stay.

The arrival

It was close to time to have our little girl. Willie, my step son, was ten and anxious to see the baby. I started labor very early one morning, and I was still having pains when it was time for Willie to go to school. Still, I made him breakfast, but then realized it was time for me to go to the hospital. Bill made Willie go to school, and he and I left for the hospital at nine in the morning. I had our daughter, Ashley Alexis Wolters, around eleven o'clock that morning, and Bill stayed in the room during the birth. Kimberly and one of my friends came to see us immediately, and when Ashley and I went home the next day, Willie came to help bring her home. Bill and Willie picked us up from the hospital in a limousine! Willie was so excited about the baby that he wanted us to take her home in style. We stopped at McDonalds in honor of Willie, the new big brother, and made a few other stops to show off the baby. We were all quite tired by the time we got home, but still we had more friends and relatives come to visit us.

I continued to run my beauty shop and work in the office, while Bill took care of Ashley most of the time. We did hire a housekeeper to clean and help take care of Ashley during the day, though. Her name was Arlene and she was a Godsend for us. She worked very hard and was also very good with our baby. While I was pregnant with Ashley, I had told Bill that I wanted her to look like him, but he insisted that little girls were ugly when they looked like their dads. But he was wrong—Ashley looked like him and she was beautiful. Bill was quite proud of her, but worried that people would think he was her grandfather. And that did happen from time to time.

I worked in my beauty salon for another couple of years, and then decided it was time for me to stay at home and work solely in the office. This was partly motivated because everywhere we would go together, Ashley would hang on this 6'2" man, and I didn't like that. After all, I was the mommy and she should be hanging on me, I thought. (Well, isn't that how you see it?)

When Ashley was four, we put her into daycare. That was good for her except that she started sucking her thumb and doing what other little kids do—like acting like a child. Up to that point, she had been mostly around adults, and she was a little Shirley Temple with bouncy curls all over her head. Her brother Willie loved her dearly, and they got along well, even though they were born ten years apart. Her big sister, Kimberly, was always there to take care of her if I needed her. They were her siblings that were around her the most, but of course, she was also around the others occasionally.

We finally got some grandchildren. Kimberly had a little boy two years after Ashley was born, and my son Jeff and his wife had a little girl soon after that. So Ashley was the star of the children, they all loved their young Aunt Ashley! They all played and had such fun together.

Things change
About that same time, my stepfather had a stroke. He and my mom lived in Guerneville, and my mom was a nurse there. Life changes when things like that happen, as you know. My mom couldn't work, and I couldn't concentrate on work in the office, so I went to be with her. Bill had decided before then that he was going to build "granny" quarters on our property for my mom and step-dad to live in. That was an exciting thought for me as I would have my mom closer.

As it turned out, my step-dad needed around-the-clock care, and my mom had no one to help with him, so finally I asked Bill if they could stay with us until their little house was done. Bill said to me, "How would you like it if I brought my parents to live with us?" Naturally, that was a reasonable question and, of course, it usually isn't healthy for parents to move in with their kids. I understood what he meant, but he let me bring them into our home anyway. That was not an easy living arrangement, and my step-dad was not an easy person in his condition. He did have to go to therapy, plus we had therapists come in the home. It was hard on everyone. We set up a hospital bed downstairs for him, and every day was an interesting day. Willie wasn't very happy with the situation, and my little Ashley even asked me one day if I loved Grandpa more than her. And, it was hard on my mom, of course.

Bill was a real trooper, though, and he never fussed at me about it at all. He didn't really help do anything for my step-dad, but Bill supported me in the decision until finally one day I found a rest home for him to go to. That was definitely a good thing! My mom would go to the rest home every day to see him, and it was so much easier for all of us. Finally the little house was ready, and Mom was so excited to move into it. It was very cute!

Arlene was still working for us, and she and my mom became good friends. That was a big help for me, as Mom didn't need to rely on me as much.

We bought a home in the Ridgemark Golf and Country Club in Hollister in 1991. It was to be our summer home since Watsonville was often foggy, and we wanted to have a little sunshine. We spent the three summer months in Hollister, and the school year in Watsonville. I always hated when we packed up and left the house for Watsonville, but our routine was to come over on weekends, so that helped a little. Even with my step-dad in the shape he was in, we took him out of the rest home occasionally to Hollister with us. We would get him out of his wheelchair into the car and head to Hollister. That wasn't an easy feat, but I guess it was worth it to me to enjoy the house I loved. As I said, Bill didn't help with anything related to my step-dad, and he just did his thing—which was usually golfing! Still, I appreciated that he didn't fuss at me over the intrusion of my parents. My mom was comfortable, and so we just dealt with what was at hand.

The ride over to Hollister could be quite interesting as my step-dad sat in the front seat, and he thought it was funny to try and open the door on his side! Talk about frustration. But, somehow we managed.

We finally quit taking my step Dad with us and let him relax in the rest home. Life was much easier. My mom couldn't see him on the weekends if she came to Hollister with us, but she had Arlene to keep her busy so that was good for all of us. Yes, life was a little easier!

My step-dad was around for a couple more years, and it was hard on my mom when he finally passed, but he was ready to go. It was hard on him being in the rest home knowing he could never go home. We did bring him home a couple of times but it was too hard on him and everyone else. He could only be there for a while during the day since my mom couldn't care for him overnight in her granny quarters, so instead we made a day of it. It had turned out to be a cute little cottage, just perfect for Mom's needs.

We had a lot of things going on in our life! The company was doing well, Bill did some traveling to see customers, and I went along occasionally, but I hated leaving my Ashley.

Ashley was involved in a lot of sports even though that wasn't really her thing, but Bill thought all kids should do every sport they could. She did track and that was her least favorite, and she was always the last one in. One day she came home, though, and was so proud to tell me that she came in second that day. Bill went to all of her events as well as Willie's. Bill told me later that day that there were only two in the race, Ashley and another girl. But she was proud!

Bill had his golf, and I had my workout that I enjoyed. Willie had his sports that he enjoyed. All in all, a pretty active family. We took summer trips with the kids, and, of course, Bill and I had our little trips together that we enjoyed.

Bill started having some cholesterol and heart issues. He loved candy, and when Ashley and I would make cookies, he would eat the raw dough before we could get them baked. He finally went to his doctor who told him he would have to quit eating so much butter and sweets, and cut out fatty food completely. Bill wasn't a very good patient, but he tried cutting down some. The doctor put Bill on heart medication, but he didn't take it like he was supposed to. He did have his nitro pills, though, and if he got uncomfortable he would take one of those. I thought he was following the doctor's orders pretty well, so I didn't always go with him when he had his medical appointments. All in all I felt comfortable enough that he was doing ok so I didn't worry much. When we went dancing, he often got a little winded, but we would sit down and he would recover quickly. So, life goes on.

Bill was in many golf tournaments, and played with his buddies a lot. I think I was what you would call a "golf widow," but I didn't mind too much as he really enjoyed it. Bill was in a big weekend tournament, and I was working in the office (of course), so I was late getting to the big victory party they had at Ridgemark that evening. Bill had won big, and all of the men would bet with each other, so Bill had won a fair amount of money on wagers. He was quite excited about winning the tournament. That evening our friend, David Taveris, told me that Bill had been complaining about his arms being uncomfortable, and naturally David was worried.

Bill, Ashley, and I sat in the hot tub that night until about two in the morning talking. I told Bill what David had said, and he promised me that first thing Monday morning he would get in to see the doctor. He didn't seem too concerned. Of course, knowing Bill, he wouldn't have told me even if he WAS worried. We had a great time chatting that evening, just enjoying a really nice end to an exciting day. Ashley never got to stay up that late, but since it was a Friday night, we thought it was ok for once.

Trouble
We were supposed to go with his parents to a party given by some of his relatives that Sunday in San Jose, after he got home from his tournament in Watsonville. I busied myself cleaning the house and getting things in order, waiting for his folks to get there. They lived down south in Atascadero, CA.

I was out washing my Corvette when I got the call. David was very calm and told me that Bill had, well, he had an accident. I knew what he meant, and I asked, "Do you mean a heart attack?" He didn't know how to respond to that. Our good friends, Teresa and Bruce, lived across the street and they were always there for us. I was panicked but trying to stay calm, all the while thinking I should put something decent on if I was going to the hospital in Watsonville. While I was trying to figure out if I could drive or not and thinking all the thoughts that go racing through your mind at such a time, my friend Teresa drove across the street and told me David had called her, and she was going to take me.

It has been 14 years ago, but it still makes my heart hurt to relive that day! Ashley stayed with our neighbor Bruce and his kids, his wife Teresa and I took off for Watsonville. I think I was on the phone calling everyone I could think of—my son, my daughter, anyone—just someone that would tell me this was just a very bad dream. Teresa would have thought I was crazy, but fortunately she was busy with her own thoughts. I really didn't want to tell my mom on the phone. I just thought I should wait and do that in person. I think I knew in my heart, though, that Bill was already gone.

When we got there, the nurse led us into a separate waiting room to talk to the doctor. It seemed like he rambled on forever before he finally spit it out! Still, I wasn't prepared to hear the news. Teresa and I just sat there, looked at one another, and cried, not knowing what to say or do. They finally took me in to see him, and it was one of the hardest things I ever had to endure. We stayed on at the hospital for a while, and then we decided to go back to Hollister. Bill's parents were there by then, and everyone was waiting for the news. That was a really hard day. Ashley took it particularly hard, but by the time my kids and grand-kids got there, she had shaken it off a little. The little kids didn't quite understand what was happening, so they were all distracted.

Ashley was only nine when her father died. Bill was only fifty-six when he passed away, and I was just fifty-four. It was a very long evening, and I had a house full of people. My mother had found out from Arlene, so Teresa and I picked her up from her little house in Watsonville, and brought her back with us to the Hollister house. As I said, the house was full of people by the end of the day. I don't know if that is good or not, but I think sometimes there can be too many. Still, of course, you want your family there with you. It was a very numbing time. Eventually most of our friends went home, and the family, except for Bill's mom and dad, and my mom.

Teresa and Bruce had earlier made sure that there was plenty of food for everyone. They were the last friends to leave and the first to be there the next morning to see what they could do.

I couldn't sleep that night, and my mom couldn't sleep either, so we sat up that night and just talked and cried. We all went back to the Watsonville house the next day where there was more room for family and friends to come and visit. That was a pretty tough time. My family and friends were very supportive of Ashley, Willie, and me, and, of course, Willie's mom and his siblings on Bill's side of the family were also very supportive of Willie.

The funeral was nice, as funerals go. We had viewing services the night before and we stayed until very late. Ashley was able to look at her father, and touch him one last time. I think that was a very healing experience. Bill looked so handsome! Many people loved Bill, and at the funeral our friend, Shari, sang and then we had several people get up and testify about what Bill meant to them, and how he touched their lives.

Now to deal
There were a lot of things to deal with. I still had a company to run, and a preteen to raise. We had an annual company meeting coming up that June, just a month after Bill's death. That was going to be hard, and my first impulse was to not go. Then I realized that was not a good idea. Our meeting was in Washington that year and the manager of that area was in charge of setting everything up, so I felt I had to go. But first I had to go shopping for some new suits. I had lost a lot of weight in just the short time from Bill's death and the meeting. I was horrified as I shopped about all of the weight I had lost. Our regional manager's wife went shopping with me and Kimberly to get ready for the trip. The meeting went quite well and everyone was very supportive. Our office manager

at the time went to the meeting with me so everything ran smoothly with all the area managers and wives that were there. We had a successful meeting with everyone's help.

There was still much to do and sort out. We had good people in all the right places who made everything run smoothly. At that meeting we talked about changing the company name from Wolters Communication to Woltcom, Inc. Bill had been talking about doing that for quite a while, trying to make the company sound more professional. We all liked the idea, and at the next board meeting we made the change.

Ashley had some dealing with things of her own. When she went back to school, I set up an appointment for her to see a school counselor. With God's help and that of the counselor, Ashley was able to deal with her grief. I checked with him quite often to see how it was going with her. Ashley went to him for two years, but finally in the third year she came to me, and told me she didn't need to see him anymore. So she quit going, and seemed fine. The counselor asked me if I needed to talk with him, but I felt I had God, and that should get me through. If you would ask me about this today, I would advise you to go to a grief counselor and just talk. It could help lessen the hurt a lot more. Of course, God saw us through many things and is still there for us.

Kimberly and my grandson moved in with us that year so that we wouldn't have to deal with things alone, and it was such a help in our life. She was separated at the time, so it was good for both of us, and the kids enjoyed each other a lot. We would still come to the Hollister house on weekends and spend summers here. Ashley and I wanted to live in Hollister, so my oldest son and his family moved into the Watsonville house while we lived here.

Mona's Story

Kimberly started working in the company, and I wanted her to eventually become the office manager.

I belonged to the "nine hole" group at Ridgemark, but after Bill's death, I didn't really have time for that luxury. "Too much to do," I'd say. But, I did continue working out when I could. You can never give that up.

My office manager at the time, Gayle, was a big help in the office. I was really numb for quite some time and couldn't concentrate. As time went on, though, I got a little more oriented and took on the responsibility of making things better. I decided to move our office into town, which was Watsonville at the time. We were all so happy that we designed the office the way we wanted it, and even added a few more people to our staff. The company was growing, and we were moving ahead. We were in that office for several years, and Kimberly was advancing in her position. Not office manager yet, but working toward it.

The kids were all growing, and Kimberly had remarried, had a little girl, and she and her husband lived in San Jose. Ashley and I were doing fine. And I had moved my mom to Hollister where she lived in an apartment. It was good for her to have her own space, and we had ours, even though we saw each other nearly every day. My mom was not the healthiest person, but we still did things together and had fun. She did her share of keeping me busy, though.

Kimberly and I had to travel to Watsonville each day for work, and it was hard for her having children in school in Hollister and having to travel thirty minutes each way. But we managed. Ashley was going to school at South Side in Hollister and I would come home and pick her up or my mother would sometimes until she got too sick to drive.

I was going through down town Hollister one day and saw the Klauer Building going up. I was sad they took out the area for our Christmas trees, but then I liked the way the building was looking. Ooh, that was exciting! I decided to go up and see if they had a space open for our company, and it so happened they did. I didn't tell anyone yet what I was up to, but I signed the lease, went to the office the next day, and called a meeting to announce the good news.

Now, if you knew me, I am not usually the type to do something big on my own without discussing it with someone else first. I figured people would try to talk me out of it, telling me many reasons why we shouldn't do that, but I wasn't going to be talked out of this. I already had the interior design in the works and someone to oversee it.

Well, when I dropped that bit of information the room was quite silent for a few minutes. Everyone was quite shocked and rightly so! Oh, well!

I got some negative feedback, and I understood it would be hard for some to commute, but it was time for a change, and Kimberly and I could both work in town, and she could be close to the kids school when they needed her.

It took quite a bit of time to make the move since there is a lot involved in packing up an office full of equipment. We were the corporate office, though, so our office could be located anywhere. I don't think I mentioned that by then our company was nationwide, and we have offices in many different states.

My office manager was having a hard time with the move, but a few others relocated to Hollister to be closer. They didn't have homes of their own, so relocation worked out well for them. Others stayed in Watsonville and commuted. Eventually

Kimberly took over the office manager position, and Gayle moved on to other business opportunities.

More bumps
Before we moved the office, my mother became very ill and passed away before she could see the new office. That was tough for me. No matter how prepared you are, you are never ready enough for any death.

I had my battles with everything and everyone goes through things in their own way. I had the close support of my oldest daughter and my friends to make it through the day when it was hard. Ashley was there for me, but a little too young to understand all that I was going through, but she was always thoughtful. Your children always want to think that you are strong, and can handle whatever comes. Ashley being a teenager had her own young life going on.

Time heals
As time goes on, you get through things and can heal somewhat, but I don't think you ever get over the passing of someone you love. I still miss Bill, and my feeling is that I really liked him, and wasn't ready for him to go. We had our ups and downs, like any marriage, but for the most part we had a great life together. I never got bored with him, and we had a lot of fun and good times together.

My mom could be a challenge, but she was my mom and I loved her, and I did my best to take care of her as a daughter should.

Today my Ashley is a married woman of one year, and very happy. At her wedding, she had a special chair for her Dad beside me, with a rose and a cigar placed on it. After all, he either chewed or smoked his cigars. That was him, and I always think of Bill when I smell cigar smoke. My Kimberly is still working hard in the company, and doing a great job.

About me
As for myself, I am pretty much retired, and only doing things as needed in the office. I never gave up working out, and I have even gotten a little more dedicated in my workouts. Along with a couple of other gals in our gym, I have done a couple of Miss Figure competitions. That is a lot of work. It is definitely a challenge, but it's kind of fun to see what your body can do (if that's what you're into). One thing Bill always did was to encourage me to work out, even when we were out of town. I may do one more competition, just for the fun of it. I'd like to do a Miss Fitness. It's a little different from Miss Figure.

So, here I am at sixty-nine-years of age and still trying to figure what I want to be when I grow up. We are never through learning and growing.

Here is how I see it, as long as I am healthy, I will enjoy life to its fullest. I enjoy my kids and grand-kids, I have two little dogs that are my newest babies and a big part of my life. I have good friends that I enjoy, and I still manage to find time to volunteer at Hazel Hawkins Hospital. I meet a lot of wonderful people there and enjoy it very much.

Some advice
I believe that you should always keep God in your life, and when you experience a death that is devastating, you should be sure to seek counsel for as long as it takes. Listening to others' hurts and how they overcame them is very important.

Take your time getting rid of your loved one's things. Keep what you think helps you until you are ready to let go. I had people try to tell me what I needed to do. It isn't their life it is your own, so do what is right for you.

I am grateful to be able to share this experience with you. Thank you, Renette, for inviting me to be a part of this wonderful sharing experience.

Chapter 10

Velma's Story

Getting to Know Us

I've always felt truly blessed that Charlie and I had such a wonderful and loving marriage, because like many couples we had almost totally different personalities. He was friendly and outgoing and could always be counted on to pop out with a funny, appropriate remark that made everyone laugh, while I tended to be painfully shy and quiet. I remember on one of our first dates, he told me seriously that I was completely deficient in the art of "making small talk." Of course during the 51 years of our marriage, he taught me that "art" so well that I'm sure that there were many times that he wished I would just "shut up." Also, Charlie, like his Mom, was somewhat of a perfectionist with quite a dominant personality. While I was flexible and easy-going and always the peace-maker—I hate the word "wishy-washy"—maybe that was me. I'm sure some of these differences had developed because of the totally different environments in which we'd each grown up.

Charlie was definitely a "small town kid"—he and his older brother had fine childhoods, were raised very properly and somewhat indulgently by a perfectionist mother and a witty, fun loving dad in the little town of Hollister, CA. They attended local schools, worked afternoons in their father's gas station, and spent every summer hiking and fishing near the family cabin in the Sierras. After high school, both boys went off to Stanford and then into the Navy during the war.

I remember being totally shocked when Charlie told me that he had never been out of California until he joined the Navy. It was so completely different for me, since by the time I was twelve, I had been completely around the world—a typical Air Force brat.

Both my younger brother and I were born in California, and I even started school in San Francisco when Daddy was stationed at Crissy Field. But then we shipped off on a big Army transport to spend the next three years in the Philippine Islands. Our three months' journey back to the States was a fairytale trip of visiting the Monkey Temple in Bali, riding elephants in Bombay, riding a camel out to the pyramids in Egypt, traveling through the beautiful tulip fields in Holland, and finally celebrating my twelfth birthday in London. I know that some of my shyness was inherited from my mother—even though she was very loving and sweet, she was quite timid and always fearful of what others would think if we didn't behave properly. Also, having to change schools and leave good friends and make new ones was always hard for both my brother and me. Thankfully, my Dad's next station in San Antonio, Texas, lasted all through our teen years and the war and even through the two years I spent at Stephens College for Women in Missouri. When I look back, it seems truly amazing that Charlie and I ever met.

I have always felt that it was "fate" that when I was a senior at Stephens and was thinking about where I would finish college, I just happened to overhear two classmates talking about going to Stanford. I'd never heard of it, but when I learned that Stanford was a very well-known University in California and that they had just banned sororities (the thought of rushing had always scared me to pieces), I decided sight-unseen that Stanford was where I wanted to go. Such a wonderful decision, because that's where I met my dear husband Charlie.

It certainly wasn't love at first sight—no bells or whistles. My first impression of him was just about the way my roommate, who had dated him early on, described him: "A really nice guy, kind of cute, with curly hair and big ears." He wasn't what you'd call handsome, but he was tall and good-looking in a boyish way, and she was right, he did have BIG ears. I have to confess that when each of our children was born I always looked first to see if they had inherited their father's ears, and later on I remember telling Charlie that his genes couldn't have been very strong because all three of our children had nice small ears and fairly straight hair. Luckily, when Charlie matured and his face filled out, somehow his ears fit better, and he became quite a good-looking man. Or maybe, by then I'd grown to love him so much that was how he looked to me.

We dated for the rest of our senior year, and I really got to know what a wonderful person he was. He was so easy to be with, and going to all the fraternity parties, dances, and football games with all our mutual friends was always great fun. One thing really impressed me, and made him "special." Charlie was an Engineering major and I was trying to finish my major in organic chemistry, and unlike other boyfriends, he was so understanding and supportive that he didn't mind a bit spending some evenings just drinking hot chocolate and helping me study for exams. Somehow, falling in love with Charlie just seemed to come naturally, and in the spring when he took me down to Hollister to meet his family, I was thrilled and excited to accept his fraternity pin and became unofficially engaged. When my Mom and Dad came for graduation, they got to meet their future son-in-law for the first time, and we had a wonderful engagement party to make it all official! We were married the following February in the beautiful little chapel in the Presidio of San Francisco (where I'd been born!).

After graduation, like most of our friends, we went to the "City" (San Francisco) to find jobs. Charlie lived in a boardinghouse, and found a job with a construction company, while I went to work in the Pharmacology Department of the Stanford Lane Hospital doing cancer research; I lived with my family in the East Bay (my father retired just after I graduated, and he and my mother had happily moved back to their home state of California.)

Happiness is being married
After a brief honeymoon, we happily settled into our first home—a small apartment in the City fairly close to the Stanford Hospital where I worked. But the very next year we moved "down the Peninsula" to Millbrae, just before the birth of our darling baby son, Bill. Then thirteen months later (my mother really raised her eyebrows, but Charlie's mom couldn't say a word because her sons were also only thirteen months apart), a darling daughter, Susan, arrived, and our little family settled into another new home. We had bought a small house in a new residential section of San Mateo, surrounded by dozens of other small houses filled with young married couples just like us. It was a happy neighborhood—hard-working Dads and stay-at-home Moms and LOTS of babies and young children. We made wonderful new friends there, had great block parties, and shared babysitting with each other. Three years later, we were blessed with another darling baby boy, Bobby. Our move to Hollister happened a year and a half later and was definitely supposed to be a temporary one. Charlie had decided to change companies, and we both decided that while he was looking, we would go back to his hometown and help his Dad with the family business.

Velma's Story

"Temporary" was definitely the wrong word—Hollister was the place we were destined to spend the rest of our lives!

What ultimately turned out to be the best decision we ever made started out with rather difficult adjustments for both of us. Charlie had loved being an engineer—removing old street car tracks from the streets in San Francisco, repaving some of the runways at the airport, and dashing off to the mountains to bid on a tunnel job were all so exciting, so to suddenly find himself working with his father in an automobile dealership in a really small town was quite a let-down, to say the least. And for me, the "world traveler," who had spent summers while I was at Stanford exploring our beautiful capitol city (Daddy had been transferred to the Pentagon at that time, and my parents were living in Washington, DC), who had visited West Point where my brother was a cadet, and who'd even attended a reception at the White House, the change was pretty drastic. When we arrived, the population of Hollister was only 8,000 and there were only 16,000 people living in the whole county! On top of that, my rather difficult mother-in-law lived just around the corner, and I knew that my greatest challenge would be living up to her very high standards and expectations. She was such a perfectionist, and I'm sure she still wasn't convinced that I was the "perfect' wife for her darling boy or the "proper" mother to raise her precious grandchildren. If the children got colds, she was right there to tell me that it was surely because I'd let them go barefooted or off to school without a proper wrap. Thank goodness, dear Charlie was always there on my side to make me feel better and soothe my "ruffled feathers". Somehow over the years, I learned to ignore the little put-downs and implied criticisms, and she finally began to appreciate me, and in the end we became really good friends who loved and respected each other.

In spite of the great change the move to Hollister made in our lives, in no time at all we began discovering all the wonderful advantages of living in our little town in the country. Charlie, his mom and dad, paternal aunts and uncles, and his formidable grandmother seemed to know almost every one in town, and most of the county, so we had no trouble getting acquainted and fitting right into a busy social life with lots of Charlie's boyhood friends, and all the other young Hollister couples we met. My teenage son once told me in great frustration that Hollister was the "end of the world," but actually it was an easy drive to parties and football games in the Bay Area, occasional trips to the City, and it was only three hours from our wonderful old cabin in the Sierras. And it was a great place to raise children (our two sons even brought their families back, so most of our grandchildren have been raised here, too!). Charlie worked very hard to learn the automobile business—never his favorite vocation—but the happy side was that now he had time and lots of energy to devote to community projects. I was always so proud of him because he somehow just knew how to make things happen.

During Charlie's 20 years on the School Board, many bond issues were passed, and new schools were built. He was one of the leaders in raising funds and building the new community Hazel Hawkins Hospital, where he served on the Board of Directors for 24 years. There's a lovely stone fountain in the garden of the new convalescent hospital dedicated to his memory. He even managed to organize the members of our golf club so that we could sell 11 million dollars worth of shares in order to purchase our Golf and Country Club from the developer. I was always busy and happy, too, helping the children with school projects, and like Charlie, getting involved in Hollister activities. Charlie's mother taught me how to can (with all the beautiful fruit and produce grown in our little valley, canning was an expected activity). I joined clubs, volunteered at the hospital, and even learned to play golf so my "Golf Nut" husband wouldn't leave me at home.

Later, after our children had all finished college and grad school, Charlie talked about selling the dealership, but he never really wanted to retire, so passing the dealership on to our youngest son was a perfect solution. Besides, we could continue living in our dear little (actually now much bigger) town, which in spite of all the beautiful places we'd visited, was still the only place we ever wanted to live.

I truly believe that what made our marriage always so loving and happy was that, in spite of our initial differences, the underlying values we'd been brought up with were just the same, and even our different personalities seemed to compliment each other. Sometimes Charlie would get worried and concerned about the business, but since I'm such a total optimist, I could almost always manage to cheer him up and get him to see the bright side. I was also able to accept the fact that he was the dominant one in our marriage, and was willing to play "second fiddle," because I knew how much he truly loved me and would do anything I really wanted. And most important of all, we were always "best friends"—we loved raising our children together, traveling together, listening to music together, golfing all over the world together, and spending summers fishing and hiking together with our children in the Sierras.

Coping with cancer
Charlie's illness seemed to come completely "out of the blue." He was always so strong and healthy and almost never missed a missed a day of work. He had a wonderful physique with big muscular arms and legs which always kind of turned me on. I, on the other hand, was forever the smallest one in my class and such a pipsqueak ("petite" is a nicer word). Dad had long skinny legs with big knobby knees, and was kind of a

disaster in shorts! Charlie, on the other hand, had grown up swimming and playing lots of tennis, so he looked great in a bathing suit. And he was always so active. Sometimes I love to curl up with a good book, but Charlie never sat around. When he wasn't in the office, he was always out gardening or playing a few holes of golf.

His first sign of trouble came right after we'd returned from a cruise down the coast of the Yucatan Peninsula. He'd had a mysterious bout of high fever on the trip which cleared right up with antibiotics, but two weeks later he landed in the hospital with bacterial pneumonia. The doctor was curious especially when he found that Charlie was also fifty percent anemic, so he ordered extensive blood tests and then a bone marrow biopsy. I can still picture that day, with the young oncologist we'd just met sitting on Charlie's bed and giving us the terrible news. Charlie had multiple myeloma, a rare and incurable form of bone marrow cancer. It's very slow growing with no early symptoms, and Charlie had probably had it for quite a few years. The prognosis was not completely devastating; without a remission, he probably had five years left. Amazingly, the doctor was completely accurate in his estimation—Charlie died exactly five years and one month later.

I really admired my dear husband so much because he didn't give an inch to the disease, and he was adamant about not telling anyone about his problem except for our family and a few very close friends. Since he looked and felt well most of the time, his golfing buddies and almost all his friends never guessed he was ill. Even his treatment wasn't too invasive. His oncologist was wonderful; he tried all the experimental drugs—incredibly expensive shots, then huge doses of prednisone, and finally chemo which was administered through a port in his chest with a little pump he could carry in his back pocket while he played golf or whatever. The chemo only made him really sick once, so we were even able to travel and carry on our normal life together. Of course, we both hoped and prayed that a new magic drug would be discovered or that he would go into remission, but sadly about six months into his into his fourth year, he finally had to give up his beloved game of golf. Little tumors caused by the cancer had invaded his back and ribs, so it was just too painful to play.

Up to this point in his illness, my role had just been to accompany Charlie to all of his doctor's appointments, watch over his medications and chemo treatments, and try as hard as I could to cook him special mouth-watering meals since chemo does terrible things to your taste buds. Hardest and most frustrating of all, was trying to keep track of all his drug and medical bills plus deal with a reluctant insurance company that was completely suspicious of all experimental drugs and treatments. Once it took me over two years of resubmitting paper work and data to finally get reimbursed for one set of expensive shots. It seemed to be a constant battle until finally our dear daughter helped me get a wonderful "insurance advocate" who effectively and efficiently handled all of Charlie's new treatment approvals. Luckily, years before, we had signed up for a "Catastrophic Illness Policy" with AFLAC, a company for which I have nothing but the highest praise (I love their duck, too.). Right after Charlie died, I was totally nonplussed to receive a call from their representative saying that they OWED me money! And she kindly took my whole box of bills to sort through and then sent me a very sizeable check!

If the first four and a half years of Charlie's illness were relatively easy, the last six months were the total opposite—completely awful. I often thought about our marriage vows, and how as a naïve young couple we'd promised to love and cherish each other "for better or worse, in sickness and in health, till death do us part." I knew I was going to love and cherish Charlie forever, but I never could have imagined this kind of "worse." He didn't want help from anyone but me, so overnight I became nurse and caregiver. I held his head when he threw up, mopped up after accidents, and even became quite good at giving enemas (the sad thing about most strong painkillers is that they also cause severe constipation). I knew that all this loss of dignity was especially hard for Charlie, but he was so brave and almost never complained, and insisted on getting up and getting dressed every single day, even the day before he died. The myeloma had leached all the calcium from the bones in his back and ribs, so finding effective pain medication was our number one priority; we visited every pain clinic in the area, but nothing ever gave him much relief. For me the hardest and most devastating thing was to have to watch him slowly disintegrating and to see my husky six-foot, 190 pound husband shrink down to just a 140-pound shadow of himself. I couldn't even hug him any more because it hurt him so much. I remember one particularly miserable evening when we both just started laughing at the total frustration of it all, and that's when he said "Honey, why don't you just take me out and shoot me." And that's when I knew that life for him was no longer worth living. Thankfully, not long after that, I asked my son (during all of those months, I don't know how I could have survived without the help and support of our wonderful children) to spend the night with us because I just somehow knew it was going to be a bad one. And it was—at three in the morning, Bill and I took Charlie to the Emergency Room for his final losing battle with pneumonia. Bill, Susie, Bob, and I were all there with him in ICU the next afternoon when he died.

During those last months, Charlie had managed to survive two other near-fatal bouts of pneumonia, and the doctor had warned me then that there was no way he could live through a third one. But as much as I thought I was prepared for Charlie's death, I still wasn't ready when it actually happened.

Velma's Story

It was suddenly SO devastatingly final with no hope left and no chance of a reprieve. Still I had to be thankful that for dear Charlie the battle was finally over and he no longer had to suffer.

The next day when reality had begun to set in, two curious things happened—one really sad and one that made us all laugh. Every morning looking out of my kitchen window, I had been greeted by a pretty pair of doves sitting on our fence, but the morning after Charlie died, sadly there was only one dove there to greet me—another loved one had been lost. That afternoon, though, we all cheered up when our small town evening paper came out with the silliest heading on a column on the front page: "Auto Mogul Dies." Honestly! We all agreed that even Charlie must be laughing at that because never in his wildest imagination would he have ever considered himself an "auto mogul!"

Laughing is one of the things I love about our family; even in the saddest circumstances, we can always find something to laugh about. I also realized how very fortunate I was to have the love of my dear children and grandchildren and all my wonderful friends who surrounded me with support and comfort. Bill, Susie, and Bob completely took over and handled everything that had to be taken care of. They planned a beautiful memorial service with Charlie's favorite classical music and songs, and even (everyone laughed) the rousing music of the Stanford Band. There was also a lovely guitar piece composed and played by our grandson, Todd. It was truly a wonderful and happy celebration of Charlie's life—I know how pleased he would have been. Charlie had been very well known in Hollister, but I was totally unprepared and completely overwhelmed by the outpouring of love and sympathy from all his friends, employees, old Stanford buddies, and dealership friends from out of town. Over 400 people tried to crowd into the church, and then so many came to visit at our house afterwards. When I expressed my gratitude and amazement, someone simply explained, "but everyone loved Charlie," One sweet youngster even told me, "There's going to be a hole in Hollister without Charlie."

Becoming an independent woman
I know that dealing with grief is a very personal and individual experience. Perhaps when Charlie was so ill, I had already done some of my grieving in just realizing that I was losing him a little every day. I missed him terribly at first, but people kept dropping in and all the lovely letters and phone calls I received were such a comfort, too. All except one, that is—I was really shocked to get a sympathy call from one widowed friend who went on and on for at least half an hour about how lonely and hard it was going to be, and how I'd never again hear from friends who'd known us as a couple. What heart-warming news that was! Ironically that call turned out to be one that really helped me. I knew that I would always be sad that I had lost my dear husband, but if, like this friend whose husband had died years before, I kept my grief front and center so that it was the first thing I thought about every morning and the last thing I thought of every night before I went to sleep, I would never be able to move on. Instead, if I thought of my life as a book that still hadn't ended, I could easily see that I had just come to the end of the chapter called "My Happy Married Life," so the best thing I could do now was to open the book to the chapter on "Becoming an Independent Women."

Happily, the calls I got from my other widowed friends were full of good tips and advice and not gloomy at all. One called to say that after her husband died she had read a whole book for widows and the one tip that she used the most was: Right equals tight and left equals loose. I know this sounds silly and simplistic, but there are so many times this has helped me change a tight light bulb or unscrew a hose nozzle or deal with one of those sticky jam jar lids. Another friend's advice was: Never turn down an invitation. This is more difficult because sometimes you just don't feel like going out, but force yourself to because you definitely need to get away from your sad lonely house and be among people again. I really had to steel myself when I went back to the Ladies' Golf group just two weeks after Charlie died because I knew that with every hug and word of sympathy an emotional rush would have me on the verge of tears again. But the good news is that you just have to go through this once per friend and then you're just part of the group again. One woman I met that first day said "Oh, Velma you're so brave to come so soon. I spent the whole first year just staying home by myself." How very sad to lose a whole year of your life!

One piece of advice was recommended by everyone: Stay busy. Go back to doing all the outside activities that you enjoyed before your husband got sick—even the ones that you had done together. Charlie and I had loved to travel, so I found friends to go with and just kept going to places we hadn't had a chance to see. Somehow I could never get my whole busy family organized for a trip together, so instead I had lovely trips to Spain and France and Japan with each family separately. And a few years ago just the ladies (my daughter, two daughters-in-law, and two granddaughters and I) spent a wonderful, happy week together in Maui to celebrate both of my granddaughters' graduations from college.

Trying something completely new and different may be a bit scary to start with, but it can also be very exciting and rewarding. I found that I really liked working with my sons and our CPA and our investment banker trying to handle all the complications that Charlie's death had created in our two family-owned businesses, the automobile dealership and our school bus company. Voila! Velma T, the new latter day "Business Woman!" I also remembered how much I'd enjoyed drawing in high school, so I joined an art class; I'll never be another Grandma Moses, but it is fun, plus now I have a whole new circle of friends. Volunteering is another great way to make new friends. Churches, hospitals, and libraries always need new volunteers and nothing makes you feel as good as knowing that you are doing something to help someone else. Actually, in looking back over the years since Charlie died, I have loved and looked forward to spending time with my children and grandchildren and it's such a comfort to have them nearby whenever I need help, but I think that my learning to share my life and activities with all my dear friends has been the most important key to finding happiness again.

I can't believe that I've almost finished my whole story without once mentioning how important and comforting my pets have been in my new life. Both Charlie and I loved animals, so all through our 51 years of marriage we were almost never without a dog and at least one or two cats. And after he died I was never really alone because our lovely and devoted golden retriever became my constant companion and security blanket. Even being alone at night wasn't scary—Scotty was right there beside my bed to keep me safe. If you've never had a pet, you can't believe how comforting it is to come home, not to a sad empty house, but to a happy, wagging tail or a soft kitty rubbing against your ankles. Plus you have a warm body to hug and love who will give you his absolute and unconditional love in return. And now that I have my darling Labradoodle, Darby, I get lots of good exercise walking her, and we often spend afternoons with another new group of friends at the dog park.

Charlie had always said that he hoped I would marry again. And sometimes when I was feeling especially lonely and in need of hugs, I thought about maybe meeting another "Prince Charming" and falling in love all over again. But as time went on and I looked around a bit, I realized that chances of finding someone as wonderful as Charlie was really very slim. Now I have definitely decided that I am completely happy and satisfied to have had one "great love of my life." Besides, having to deal with an old "Prince," no matter how "Charming," somehow doesn't seem appealing at all. My days are full and satisfying, and there are always friends to call or visit, and even new adventures to look forward to. It's been 11 years since I lost Charlie, and I can truthfully say that I'm really happy and content living this new chapter of my life as an Independent Woman.

There's just one more thing to add—I've really learned to appreciate the wisdom of that outstanding woman, Helen Keller, who said, "When one door of happiness closes, another opens, but often we look so long at the closed door that we do not see the one that has been opened for us." And my wish for all the widows who read this book is that each of you will be able to find your own new door of happiness.

Inner Views
Renette Torres

After the grieving period, I can promise you, your life will go forward . . . but you have to make the effort. Below is your check list. When you look over this list, check off the lines that you have been successful at, and then work on the hard ones that are left. *YOU can do it!*

- [ ] Surround yourself with people who like to laugh. No grouches! No downers!
- [ ] Remember, laughter is contagious. It makes everyone feel good.
- [ ] Try to have lots of friends . . . preferably younger than you—both guys n' gals!
- [ ] Never be around people who are negative or who constantly complain.
- [ ] Always keep a positive, upbeat attitude.
- [ ] Keep life simple. The more complicated, the more stress.
- [ ] I am a jokester, and I love to make people laugh. You try it!
- [ ] Exercise your body. More importantly, exercise your brain.
- [ ] Write your memoirs, if not for the world, for your family.
- [ ] Enjoy your life alone or with others. Life is what YOU make it.

- [ ] Don't worry about tomorrow, it'll be here before you know it.
- [ ] Feeling alone? Call a friend to go shopping or have lunch.
- [ ] When you feel down (it happens even to me, and I'm always up), play with your dog. He'll make you laugh. You don't have one? Get one!
- [ ] Invite your friends to a luncheon or dinner party, play cards, or show old movies.
- [ ] Always think of new and fun things to do. Be creative.
- [ ] Do you feel sorry for yourself? Quit it! In a funk? Get out of it!
- [ ] Go outside, look up at the sky and know HE is looking down on you.
- [ ] The only time you should look back is to recall the great memories you have.
- [ ] Look at photographs or watch videos and hear him talking to you.
- [ ] Do you like cooking? Try a new recipe.
- [ ] Lonely? Go online to a "match" venue to meet someone, but be careful, there are lots of creeps out there. Be sure you have coffee in a public place first.
- [ ] It may be hard, but try to be happy, laugh at yourself, and have a positive attitude.
- [ ] If you're down in the dumps, you wallow by yourself! It's up to YOU.
- [ ] Last, but not least, always wear a smile on your face . . . it'll make people wonder what you've been up to!

About the Authors

This is the second book for **Renette Torres.** A successful entrepreneur who started up her own watch and clock company, she is a world traveler, avid golfer, and at 83 is as lively and energetic as her rambunctious dog, Bogie, enjoying life in Hollister, CA.

Also contributing is her granddaughter, **Courtney McEntee**, who is currently pursuing an accounting degree at a college in Southern California, and looking forward to a financial career following her grandfather's footsteps.

Lynn Nilsen lives in Santa Cruz, CA, and enjoys skiing, golf, hiking with her dog, and spending time with family and friends. She owns and manages commercial real estate.

Living in beautiful Monterey, CA, **Shirley Chapman** is sliding down the second half of her bell curve, still an adventurous survivor, and seeing opportunity in every challenge.

continued . . .

 A native of Germany, **Helma Smith** arrived in San Francisco in 1962 to follow a dream. She experienced the death of two very different spouses, one deliberate, and the other spontaneous. She lives in Seaside and still works part-time in the same office after nearly 50 years.

 **Marlene "Marty" Bolla** lives in Gilroy, CA. Having survived a troubled marriage, she still works in a major cardiac hospital in San Jose and spends her free time with her hobbies, biking, and socializing with her friends.

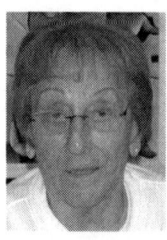 As a young Jewish girl, **Stefi Rudolph** fled Nazi Germany in 1939 with her parents and sister. Following the death of her husband, she retired from the family business after several more years, and still lives in the San Francisco Bay Area.

 **Becky Funk**, was raised in San Francisco. She enjoys Mah Jongg and card games, and still sells real estate in the Palm Springs area.

 A native Kansan, **Mona Wolters** is "pretty-much retired" from the communications business she and her husband Bill built; she still maintains her healthy and active lifestyle through workouts and competitions.

 **Velma Tiffany** met her husband Charlie while they attended Stanford University together. Velma still loves to travel and does local volunteer work; she lives in Hollister, CA with her animals.

CPSIA information can be obtained at www.ICGtesting.com
Printed in the USA
BVOW072049030613

322312BV00002B/7/P